From DEBT to WEALTH

12 KEYS to EARN money WITH what YOU have

Toyin Obafemi

Copyright 2024 by Toyin Obafemi

Published by Pnuxel Consulting
toyin@pnuxelconsulting.com

All rights reserved. No part of this book may be reproduced or transmitted in any form or by any means- electronic or mechanical, including photocopying, recording, or by any information storage and retrieval system without the author's written permission except for the inclusion of brief quotations in a review.

I am not a certified financial expert, and the insights shared in this book are based on my personal views and experiences. While I hope these perspectives offer valuable guidance, I strongly recommend that you consult with a qualified financial advisor before making any decisions relating to your financial investment and management.

Contents

Acknowledgements 6
Introduction 7

Key One: Being A Good Person Doesn't Automatically Credit Your Account With Money 9

Key Two: Ask For A Solution And Not For Money 19
Pray To God For A Solution. 20
Stop Asking For Money But For A Solution. 27

Key Three: Convert The Idea To Valuable Assets .. 37
A Simple Guide On How To Generate Ideas 39
Conception And Misconception Of Ideas 49
A Simple Guide On How To Convert Your Ideas To Valuable Assets 57

Key Four: What Do You Have? 66
Stop Looking Outward, Start Looking Inward! 70

Key Five: What You Have Is Enough — Grow It! 83
Identify Your Seed! 85
Do Not Be Quick To Forget That You Are A Steward 89
It Is Your Duty To Identify Your Seed 99
Ideas Build Upon One Another 101

Key Six: Nothing Happens If You Do Not Act...... 104
    Work Is A Blessing.. 108

Key Seven: Cherish Your Networks And Relationships 122
    Be Honest And Trustworthy 128

    The Power Of Relationships And Integrity: A Real-Life Success Story 131

Key Eight: Understanding Bad And Good Debts. 138
    Assets And Liabilities.. 144

    Financial Freedom 146

    Using Other People's Money (OPM) for Wealth Creation 148

Key Nine: Avoid Distractions....................................... 153
    Identifying And Eliminating Distractions............ 154

    Useful Tools To Help You Eliminate Distractions. 159

    Apart From the Above, Here Is The Greatest Tool I Have Found In Eliminating Distractions.............. 162

    Guard Your Mornings... 171

    Get Away From The Crowd 172

Key Ten: You Get Results To The Extent Of Your Faith And Willingness To Take Calculated Risks 177
    Don't Be Afraid To Fail. 180

    Three Feet Away From Gold 184

    Do What You Haven't Done Before 187

Key Eleven: Be A Salesperson 190
    Don't Be Ashamed To Sell 193

    A Simple Guide To Overcoming The Fear Of Selling 196

    5 Essential Attributes Of A Successful Salesperson 198

Key Twelve: Manage Your Resources 202

Unlock Your Potential: Discover the Transformative Power of My Other Books... 208
The Author 212
References 215

Acknowledgements

First and foremost, I want appreciate God, the giver of life, opportunity and wealth. Without Him, none of this would be possible.

My deepest gratitude goes to my lovely and caring wife, Temitope, for her unwavering support and encouragement. Her belief in me is a source of motivation. Thank you.

I would also like to thank our precious children, Oreofe and Inioluwa, for being a source of inspiration. Their joy, peace and curiosity remind me of the importance of living in the present without worry and making the most of every moment.

I am also deeply grateful to Adewobi Adebanjo for going out of his way to design the cover for this book. You have always been reliable. Thank you!

Introduction

Have you ever wondered why some people seem to live in wealth while many others remain trapped in debt and poverty? Is it just fate, or did God create some to be wealthy while leaving others to struggle, living in lack and penury?

Have you also considered why and how some people seem to turn the slightest opportunity into massive success while others continue to struggle despite their efforts?

What if the difference between your current situation and your financial breakthrough lies not in luck but in your ability to leverage proven principles and maximise the resources already within your reach without necessarily looking outward for answers?

What if the solution to your financial struggles is already within your reach, but you're simply unaware of it? And what if your breakthrough is closer than you think, waiting for you to tap into it?

I have written this book, **"FROM DEBT TO WEALTH: 12 Keys to Earn Money with What You Have"**, to answer these and similar questions and to explore 12 proven strategies that will guide you to create and multiply wealth. If you truly understand and apply these keys, you will never have to worry about money again. Instead, you'll build sustainable wealth. These 12 keys are practical, actionable, and life-changing.

Let's embark on this journey together as you're about to unlock your ability to create sustainable wealth.

KEY ONE

Being A Good Person Doesn't Automatically Credit Your Account With Money

I am glad to welcome you to this journey of transformation. By choosing to read this book, you've already taken the first step toward your financial success. Whether you're currently in debt or simply looking to increase your wealth, you will be empowered with the knowledge to unlock your potential to move from debt to wealth or to grow your wealth, as the case may be. But remember, knowledge alone isn't enough—action is vital. As we go through the 12 keys in this book to creating wealth, it's crucial that you put them into practice because nothing changes unless you act. Your actions will be the catalyst for your financial transformation.

We will draw insights from the story of Elisha, the prophet and the poor widow. If you're unfamiliar with the story, here is it: "One day, the widow of a member of the group of prophets came to Elisha and cried out, "My husband who served you is dead, and you know how he feared the LORD. But now a creditor has come, threatening to take my two sons as slaves." "What can I do to help you?" Elisha asked. "Tell me, what do you have in the house?" "Nothing at all, except a flask of olive oil," she replied. And Elisha said, "Borrow as many empty jars as you can from your friends and neighbours. Then go into your house with your sons and shut the door behind you. Pour olive oil from your flask into the jars, setting each one aside when it is filled." So she did as she was told. Her sons kept bringing jars to her, and she filled one after another.

Soon every container was full to the brim! "Bring me another jar," she said to one of her sons. "There aren't any more!" he told her. And then the olive oil stopped flowing. When she told the man of God what had happened, he said to her, "Now sell the olive oil and pay your debts, and you and your sons can live on what is left over.""[1]

This chapter focuses on the first key of the 12 we'll explore in this book: *"Being a Good Person Doesn't Automatically Credit Your Account with Money."*

Being a good person is undoubtedly valuable but does not guarantee financial success. While integrity, kindness, and good moral character are essential, they do not automatically translate into wealth. You can live a life of honesty and virtue yet still struggle financially if you do not understand and apply the principles of creating wealth. Many people assume that being a good person is enough to prosper, but the reality is that wealth is built by knowledge, strategy, and action, not just good intentions. This chapter explains how important it is to use financial principles to build lasting wealth while also being a good person. This understanding will empower you on your journey to financial success.

The story of the prophet Elisha and the poor widow illustrates that being a good person doesn't automatically lead to financial success. The widow cried out to Elisha in desperation, saying, "My husband who served you is dead, and you know how he feared the LORD. But now a creditor has come, threatening to take my two sons as slaves."[1] Her husband, a man of integrity who feared the Lord, left his family in serious financial trouble. Despite his devotion, he died poor, leaving behind a debt so significant that his family faced the risk of losing their sons to slavery.

This story underscores a harsh reality: being a good person alone does not prevent financial hardship. The widow's husband was undoubtedly a good man, but his goodness did not stop his family from poverty. If being a good person was enough to secure financial prosperity, this man would have lived a wealthy life, free from the burden of debt. Unfortunately, it was the other way around. It's possible that his death, which is likely untimely, may be linked to the stress and burden of lack.

The lesson here is clear: while integrity and a solid moral compass are invaluable, they must be married with the understanding of wealth creation principles. The widow's husband may have been rich in character, but his family was left impoverished for lack of engaging wealth creation principles, which we will explore in this book. This example serves as a warning and a call to action—good character must be accompanied by wealth-creation strategies and principles to ensure your well-being and those you care about.

Can one be a good person and still be rich? Absolutely, and that is the purpose of this book. I want you to maintain high moral standards while you also achieve wealth. Acquiring wealth will amplify your good deeds because money doesn't change a person; instead, it reveals who they indeed are. If a man is wicked and gains riches, he becomes more wicked because he now has the means to amplify his values.

Conversely, if a man is good, kind, and honest, his deeds will likewise be amplified with wealth. This means that your good intentions will be dwarfed if you are poor. You do not want to stay in this position because it is not a good place to be. Strive to be like Abraham, who was both righteous and wealthy.

Can someone be wicked and still be rich? Why not?. We've seen people attain power and wealth despite having terrible characters. Some followed the principles of wealth creation, while others took what didn't belong to them through force and injustice.

While both good and bad individuals can attain wealth, the choice to walk the path of integrity is far more rewarding. If given a choice, wouldn't you prefer to be a good person and still achieve financial success? A wicked person might accumulate wealth, but they will eventually reap the consequences of their actions. In contrast, a good person not only builds wealth but also enjoys the peace of mind and satisfaction that comes with a life lived rightly.

Interestingly, integrity is not just a moral virtue; it is also a powerful asset that can be leveraged to create wealth. Money is considered a form of currency since it flows just like a current. Integrity works similarly as it can also serve as a form of currency. This shows that money is not the only form of capital for investment to create wealth. Money flows in the direction of value, and so does integrity, which opens doors for opportunities. When you maintain your integrity, you attract trust and open doors that might otherwise remain closed. People are more willing to engage with you, invest in your ideas, and offer you opportunities when they know you are a person of your word.

Integrity creates a strong foundation upon which wealth can be built. When you are known for your honesty and reliability, your reputation becomes a currency in itself. This currency can lead to business deals, partnerships, and investments that help you grow your wealth. So, while being a good person may not automatically credit your account with money, it could be leveraged as a channel to wealth inflow.

The poor prophet could have leveraged his integrity to secure his family's financial future. His integrity could have opened doors to opportunities such as business transactions, contracts, or partnerships that would have provided him with the resources needed to keep his family out of debt. All he needed was to know how to take advantage of his integrity and honesty. He might have secured a business partnership because he was trusted, which would have generated income.

In a world where trust is often hard to come by, the prophet's integrity could have been his most valuable asset. If he had been able to leverage this integrity, it might have secured him the financial stability needed to avoid the dire situation his family faced after his death. The lesson here is clear: integrity isn't just a moral obligation; it's a powerful tool that can create tangible opportunities and prevent financial hardship.

"A good man leaves an inheritance to his children's children."[2] This emphasises the importance of leaving a lasting legacy. A good man leaves both tangible and intangible assets for his children's children. For the prophet in this story, he only left behind an intangible wealth. It would have been perfect if he had left both behind. Beyond tangible wealth, a man should also leave intangible wealth, which includes integrity, love, kindness, virtue, and friendship, among other qualities.

In wrapping up this chapter, it's crucial to understand that while being a good person is commendable, it does not automatically translate into financial success. The story of the prophet who left his family in debt is a reminder that integrity and moral character, while valuable, need to be paired with financial knowledge and principles. A good man ensures that he leaves a legacy of both tangible and intangible wealth for future generations.

Moving forward to Chapter Two, we will explore Key Number Two: "Ask for a Solution and Not for Money." The next chapter will guide you on how to shift your focus from seeking immediate financial aid to finding sustainable solutions. By learning to ask for and identify the right solutions, you will discover how to create long-term wealth and financial stability. Let's dive into how this mindset can transform your financial journey.

KEY TWO

Ask For A Solution And Not For Money

The next key to consider is **"Ask for a Solution and Not for Money."** In the story we've been exploring, the woman found herself in a desperate situation—her two sons were on the brink of being taken away to serve for the family's debt. In her distress, she cried out to the prophet for help. This moment holds two important lessons. First, it reminds us of the value of seeking help when needed. We often try to handle everything independently, but asking for guidance or support can open doors to new possibilities.

Secondly, perhaps more importantly, the moment teaches us to ask for a solution, not money. When faced with financial challenges, it's easy to think that more money is the answer. However, asking for money often provides only a temporary fix. It can be likened to addressing the symptoms but not the root cause. Instead, by seeking a solution, you're thinking long-term—looking for a way to create lasting change in your financial situation. Rather than asking for a temporary relief that won't last, why not focus on finding a lasting solution that can transform your financial reality?

Pray To God For A Solution.

If you find yourself in a financial mess, I encourage you to pray to God for a solution. Just as the woman in the story sought help from the prophet, which can be seen as reaching out to the Divine, we too can turn to God in times of need. It is never out of place to ask for help from your Creator. He knows you more intimately than you know yourself and is always willing to extend His hand in assistance. All you need to do is ask. Prayer is a powerful way to seek guidance and solutions, especially when you feel overwhelmed by your circumstances. Don't forget that *"We are not human beings having a spiritual experience; we are spiritual beings having a human experience."* - Pierre Teilhard de Chardin.

It's important to remember that you don't have to suffer in silence. Financial struggles can be unpalatable, making you feel like you are carrying the world's weight on your shoulders. But you don't have to bear that burden alone. You are clearly admonished to "Give all your worries and cares to God, for He cares about you."[3] This verse is a profound reminder that God is not indifferent about your struggles. He cares deeply about you and is ready to help you navigate difficult times. So, don't hold back on your worries and cares—give them all to God because He truly cares.

How do you hand over these burdens to God? You do so by praying to Him. Prayer should not be taken as a religious exercise but as a lifeline to the Divine. It is your way of communicating your needs, fears, and desires to the One who can change your situation. When you pray, you acknowledge that you cannot do it alone and need His intervention. This act of humility opens the door for God to step in and provide you with the solutions you need.

Moreover, prayer is not just about asking for help but about building a relationship with your Creator. Through prayer, you deepen your connection with Him, allowing His wisdom and guidance to flow into your life. Through this relationship, you can gain clarity, strength, and the discernment needed to make wise financial decisions. So, don't hesitate to pray when you are in a tight spot. Trust that God will hear your prayers and respond with the solutions you need to overcome your financial challenges.

Also, when asking God for help, it's crucial to distinguish between genuine prayer and mere complaining. Many people think they are praying when, in reality, they are just venting their frustrations. There's a difference between pouring out your worries by complaining and approaching God with faith and a thankful heart. Apostle Paul wisely advises, "Don't worry about anything; instead, pray about everything. Tell God what you need, and thank Him for all He has done. Then you will experience God's peace, which exceeds anything we can understand. His peace will guard your hearts and minds as you live in Christ Jesus."[4] This teaches us that true prayer involves laying our concerns before God with gratitude, trusting that He can resolve our issues. In doing so, we open ourselves to experiencing divine peace, transcending our understanding and calming our hearts and minds.

Worrying is counterproductive, especially when it comes to finding solutions. A mind clouded by worry is often unable to focus or think clearly, making it difficult to see a way out of difficult situations. Think back to a time when you were overwhelmed with worry. Were you able to think clearly? Did solutions come easily to you, or were you stuck in a loop of anxiety and frustration? Worrying clouds your judgment and prevents you from being receptive to the guidance and ideas that could lead to a solution.

A peaceful heart, on the other hand, is a fertile ground for solutions to emerge. When you learn to hand over your worries to God without complaining, you create space for His peace to fill your mind and heart. This peace guides you toward the answers you need. In the quietness of a peaceful heart, ideas, innovations, and actionable strategies surface, offering you the way out of your financial troubles or any other challenges you may face.

So, instead of allowing worry to consume you, learn to hand over the burden to your Creator. When you feel the weight of your problems bearing down on you, take a moment to pause, pray, and thank God in advance for the solution He will and has provided. This act of faith alleviates your burden and opens the door for divine inspiration to flow into your life.

When you find yourself in a difficult situation, it's easy to fall into the trap of lamenting your circumstances. However, rather than asking, *"God, can't you see that I am poor? Don't you care that I am struggling financially? I have worked hard, but I do not have anything tangible to show for it,"* or dwelling on the severity of your problems, a shift in perspective is needed. Instead of focusing on the issue, approach God with the mindset that your challenges are opportunities in disguise. Say, *"Oh Lord, I know you permitted this so that your works might be manifested in my life. What would you like me to do? How can I navigate this situation? Show me the steps to take."* This shift from complaining to seeking divine guidance allows you to see your situation from a different, more hopeful perspective, helping you identify the solutions available. As we will see in this book, the solutions to our problems are not far away — they are closer than we might imagine. All we need is the ability to recognise and acknowledge the solutions that have always been with us.

It's important to remember that every challenge presents an opportunity for growth, learning, and eventual success. When you ask God what to do, you are inviting Him into your situation, acknowledging His sovereignty, and expressing your trust in His plan for your life. This is not just about asking for a quick fix but seeking wisdom and understanding to turn the situation around. Often, the solution God provides is not just about addressing the immediate need but also about positioning you for greater opportunities in the future.

By approaching your difficulties with this mindset, you will begin to see them as stepping stones rather than stumbling blocks. This approach empowers you to look beyond the immediate discomfort and focus on the long-term potential of the situation. You may discover that what seemed like a setback is actually a setup for a greater breakthrough. The key is to be patient, listen for God's direction, and be ready to act on the guidance you receive.

In this process, you may find yourself developing new skills, uncovering hidden talents, or even forging new relationships that will prove invaluable in the future. The opportunities that arise from your challenges can lead to avenues you never imagined. But this can only happen if you move from a mindset of despair and fear to one of faith and hope.

STOP ASKING FOR MONEY BUT FOR A SOLUTION.

When faced with financial challenges, the instinctive reaction is often to ask for money to alleviate the immediate pressure. However, simply asking for money only provides temporary relief, like treating the symptoms of an illness without addressing the underlying cause of the sickness. Instead of seeking quick fixes, it's far more effective to ask for a solution — a sustainable way out of your financial difficulties. Solutions address the root cause of the problem, offering long-term relief and the potential for lasting financial stability. So stop asking for money but for a solution. Do not pray to God for money; likewise, do not ask anyone for a quick bailout but for a lasting solution to your financial problems. This is a very important key to moving yourself from debt to wealth.

In the story we are considering, the woman cried out to the prophet in despair, likely expecting a bailout. She probably thought that if she explained her predicament to the prophet, given her late husband's good standing among the prophets, they would come to her aid. Perhaps they would raise a donation or a welfare offering to help her out of her financial mess. However, contrary to her expectations, the prophet did not raise an offering or donation for her. Instead, he took a different approach.

The prophet's response to the woman's plea is an essential lesson in seeking a sustainable solution rather than a temporary relief. Instead of providing her with the financial bailout she likely expected, he asked her: "What can I do to help you? Tell me, what do you have in the house?"[1] This question shifted her focus from what she lacked to what she already possessed. The prophet understood that the key to overcoming her financial hardship was not in receiving a one-time bailout but in identifying and utilizing the resources she already had to create a lasting solution. You need a mind-shift in this regard if you want to move yourself from debt to wealth.

This principle applies not only to individuals but also to nations. When a nation seeks only relief and not a lasting solution to its challenges, it will remain dependent and a servant. Such a nation will have a hindered development and ability to create wealth. Many developing nations fall into this trap, relying on bailouts instead of pursuing sustainable solutions. These nations may not realise that the countries now offering them aid were once in similar situations. However, they chose to tackle their problems head-on, seeking solutions rather than temporary relief. Wealth gravitates toward those who provide solutions, not those who merely beg for help. So, rather than asking for money, focus on finding solutions. It's perfectly fine to seek assistance in developing those solutions, but the goal should always be to address the root of the problem, not just the symptoms.

Many times, the solution to your problems is within your reach. You only need insight, dedication, and some effort to find it rather than seeking the easy way out. True wealth is not built on handouts or short-term fixes but leveraging what you have to create something valuable. If you take the time to seek a solution rather than opting for the quick relief of easing your financial pressure, you will discover that the solution lies within you. That's why this book focuses on showing ways to earn money with what you already have. You don't need to look outward; instead, look inward and transform what you possess into valuable assets that can attract wealth.

Imagine if the prophet had simply given her money. It might have solved her immediate crisis but wouldn't have prevented future financial struggles. By guiding her to discover and use her resources, he helped her solve her money problems once and for all. I hope you understand this point. Everyone wants the easy way out, but that is not the path to lasting success. Don't ask for money; ask for a solution.

Building on what we've discussed, it's crucial to shift your mindset from asking for money to asking for solutions. When you pray, instead of focusing on receiving cash, focus on receiving guidance, ideas, and opportunities that can lead to financial freedom. Money is a byproduct of value creation, which stems from innovative ideas, strategic actions, and problem-solving.

Consider this: when you pray for money, you are essentially asking for a temporary fix to your financial situation. However, praying for ideas and solutions opens the door to long-term wealth and sustainability. God, as the ultimate creator, doesn't deal with currency; He deals with creativity. He inspires ideas that, when acted upon, can generate wealth.

Take the story of the widow as an example. She didn't receive money from the prophet; instead, she received a solution—an idea that, when acted upon, resulted in the financial breakthrough she desperately needed. The same principle applies to us today. Rather than waiting for a miraculous rain of money, we should be attentive to the creative solutions God provides.

It's easy to overlook the power of ideas, especially when you're in the midst of a financial crisis. But remember, every successful business, innovation, and breakthrough began with an idea. The challenge lies in recognising these ideas as answers to your prayers and taking the necessary steps to bring them to life.

When you pray, do not ask God for money. Why should you ask God for money when money is not printed in heaven? There is nothing like dollars, pounds, naira, or yen in heaven. Money is printed on earth, so asking God for money is not the right way to go if you genuinely want to break free of debt.

Let me illustrate this with a scenario. Imagine you are in Nigeria, and I am in the United States. You needed financial assistance from me, and when you ask, all I can do is send you what we have and spend here in the U.S.—which is dollars. I wouldn't send naira to you because that currency isn't printed where I am. So, I sent one thousand dollars to you. When you receive it in Nigeria, the money is useless to you in its current form because the dollar is not the accepted means of exchange there. To get value from what I've sent, you need to convert the dollars into naira, the accepted currency where you live.

The same applies to God. He cannot send you money directly because money is not the currency of heaven. God is a creator and, therefore, deals with creativity and ideas. When you pray to Him for help, He responds by inspiring your mind with ideas and wisdom and helps you see opportunities you probably have not considered before. These are the currencies of heaven, and when you "convert" them by acting on them here on earth, they lead to financial breakthroughs.

People often pray with the expectation of receiving free money or some miraculous money rain. But they don't realise that God has already answered their prayers in the form of ideas or opportunities they may overlook because they were expecting something else. They keep waiting for money to fall from the sky, not realising that the answer to their financial struggles has already been given to them in the form of ideas.

Interestingly, the ideas God provides often come in the simplest and most unassuming forms. They don't arrive with the dramatic flair of thunder or a booming voice calling your name. Instead, they quietly settle in your mind as a gentle nudge, a subtle thought, or a seemingly ordinary idea. Because of their simplicity, these ideas are often overlooked or dismissed as too insignificant to be the solution to a pressing problem. Yet, it is in their simplicity that their power lies.

Many people make the mistake of disregarding these ideas because they seem too easy. They're searching for something more complex or miraculous, not realizing that the solution to their financial troubles has already been given to them in a form they can handle. The simplicity of these ideas doesn't diminish their effectiveness. In fact, it's this simplicity that makes them actionable and within your reach. Don't underestimate the quiet whispers of inspiration—they could be the very key to unlocking your financial freedom.

As we conclude this chapter on asking for a solution rather than money, it's important to remember that true wealth begins with the right mindset. Instead of seeking temporary relief or a quick fix, focus on uncovering the solutions that can lead you to lasting financial freedom. The ideas and solutions you receive are the seeds of your financial breakthrough. Your responsibility is to recognise, value, and act upon them.

This leads us to the next crucial step on your journey: **"Key 3: Convert the Idea to Valuable Assets."** It's not enough to have a great idea; you must take that idea and transform it into something tangible, something that generates value. In the next chapter, we'll explore how to take the concepts and inspirations you receive and turn them into real-world assets that add value to people and bring money and fulfilment in return to you.

KEY THREE

Convert The Idea To Valuable Assets

As we progress on this journey, building on the foundation in the first two keys, it's time to turn our focus to converting your idea to valuable assets.

Ideas alone, no matter how brilliant, remain intangible until they are acted upon. The true power of an idea lies in its ability to be transformed into something of value—something that can generate wealth and create opportunities. In this chapter, we will explore how to transform those ideas into real, tangible assets that can elevate your financial standing and set you on the path to lasting success.

What is an idea? An idea, in simple terms, is a thought, concept, or mental image that holds the potential to solve a problem, meet a need, or create something new. It's the seed of innovation—the starting point for every invention, business, or movement that has ever changed the world. However, an idea in itself has no intrinsic value until it is acted upon. The true worth of an idea is realised only when it is transformed into something that can be used.

To illustrate this, imagine a farmer who possesses a handful of seeds. The seeds have the potential to grow into crops that can feed a family, be sold in the market, or be used to produce even more seeds. However, if the farmer keeps the seeds in a jar, they remain just that—with unrealised potential. Only when the farmer plants, nurtures, and eventually harvests the crops is the value of those seeds realised.

Similarly, the ideas you generate are like those seeds. They must be cultivated, nurtured, and transformed into something tangible and valuable. Converting your ideas into valuable assets is the process of creating wealth. Without this conversion, ideas remain dormant, with their potential never fully realised.

Interestingly, each of us has a solution for the world. We possess a gift to offer, which may still be intangible. We must learn to convert these gifts from their intangible state into products and services that can benefit others. In doing so, you will find fulfilment and receive worthy compensation for your work. You will end up being paid for doing what you were created to do and love to do.

A SIMPLE GUIDE ON HOW TO GENERATE IDEAS

Ideas are the foundation of every innovation and solution. They are sparked by various factors, and understanding how they come about can help you become more intentional in generating them. Here's a simple guide to help you understand and harness the process of idea generation:

1. **Identify a Problem or Need and be willing to provide a solution:** The first step in generating an idea is recognising a problem or a need. This could be something you encounter in your daily life, something you observe in your community, or a gap in the market. *Problems create opportunities for ideas to form because they demand solutions.*

    You can never run out of ideas because problems and needs are always present. Every complaint and frustration people voice is an opportunity waiting for someone with the right mindset to seize. Instead of joining in on the complaints, train your mind to see these moments as fertile ground for idea generation. This shift in perspective is a powerful tool that can transform your financial situation, moving you from debt to wealth or further increasing your wealth by solving problems that others are facing.

Consider the evolution of communication as an example. Decades ago, sending a message to someone far away was laborious. You had to write a letter, send it through the post office, and wait days or even weeks for it to reach its destination. There was an apparent demand for a faster, more reliable communication method. This need sparked the idea that led to the development of modern communication technologies. Today, we can send a message instantly from the comfort of our homes to anyone, anywhere in the world, thanks to those who saw the problem and provided a valuable, world-changing solution. Not only did they improve the lives of countless people, but they also created a steady flow of wealth for themselves by providing solutions that people needed.

Another compelling example comes from the biblical story of Joseph in Egypt. When Pharaoh had a troubling dream about seven years of famine, it posed a significant problem. Joseph was called upon to interpret the dream, and when asked what should be done, he didn't hesitate. He didn't say, "I have no idea." Instead, he proposed a solution: during the seven years of plenty, Egypt should save twenty per cent of its harvest to prepare for the coming years of famine. This idea was so sound that Pharaoh appointed Joseph as the prime minister to oversee its implementation. Joseph's ability to generate a solution to the problem not only saved Egypt but also elevated him to a position of power and wealth. This story illustrates the importance of having ideas that solve real problems if you aspire to create wealth.

Here is another illustration as identifying a problem and need and your perspective on it are crucial to idea generation and wealth creation. It is the story of two shoe salesmen who were sent to a town. When the first salesman arrived, he saw a hopeless situation. All he noticed were poor people with no shoes, and he immediately concluded that there was no opportunity for business in the town. Discouraged, he requested to be sent back to the headquarters, believing that there was no market for shoes in such a place.

However, when another salesman was sent to the same town, he saw something entirely different. Instead of seeing a lack of opportunity, he saw an untapped potential. To him, the fact that no one had shoes meant that everyone needed them. He recognised that there was a significant market just waiting to be served. Excited by the possibilities, he requested that footwear be produced and sent to the town, confident that the demand would be high.

This story highlights the importance of how you perceive problems and needs. The first salesman saw an obstacle, while the second saw an opportunity. In the same way, when you identify a problem or need, you can view it as a potential avenue for innovation and value creation. By choosing to see opportunities where others see only difficulties, you position yourself to generate ideas that can lead to significant success. This mindshift is crucial for wealth creation.

Therefore, the first step in generating ideas is to identify a problem or need for which you are willing to provide a solution. Look around you—what are people struggling with? What needs are not being met? Start by listing 20 problems or needs in your immediate environment. These could be anything from everyday inconveniences to more significant challenges facing your community or industry.

Once you have your list, choose five problems or needs you can proffer solutions to, and brainstorm potential solutions for them. This exercise will sharpen your ability to generate ideas and set you on the path to wealth creation by positioning you as a solution provider.

Remember, wealth flows to those who solve problems, not those who complain about them. Every problem is a door to an opportunity—your task is to find the key.

2. **Gather Information:** Once you've identified a problem, immerse yourself in learning more about it. Ask people about their opinions, do a survey, research the actual need gaps, read articles about the problem, talk to experts, and gather as much information as possible. The more you know, the better equipped you are to think of creative ways to address the problem.

Gathering information is an essential step in idea generation. Understanding the problem or need from several possible angles gives you leverage to provide an effective solution. The more you expose yourself to different perspectives, the more comprehensive your understanding will become. This depth of knowledge can inspire more innovative and effective solutions.

Talking to experts is another invaluable part of this process. Experts have spent years, sometimes decades, studying or working in a particular field. Their insights can give you a clearer understanding of the challenges and existing solutions so that you don't replicate what has been done. They might even point out gaps or inefficiencies in current methods you haven't considered. Also, you could be inspired to find out why the current solution is not working or even find a way to tweak the present solution for better acceptability, efficiency, and effectiveness.

3. **Brainstorm:** Brainstorming is the process of generating as many ideas as possible without worrying about whether they are practical or feasible. Write down every thought that comes to mind, no matter how small or seemingly irrelevant. Often, great ideas are hidden within the seeds of what may initially seem like simple or even silly thoughts.

It's essential to create dedicated time for brainstorming. This is sometimes called "brain work," and it's a crucial aspect of generating new ideas. In my book, **"FIND YOUR WORK: Unlocking Your Path to Impact, Fulfilment, and Worthy Compensation,"** I delve deeper into the forms of work and how to engage them effectively. You may want to get the book for further explanation. During brainstorming, it's essential to minimise distractions, as they can hinder the flow of creative thoughts and prevent you from getting the most out of this valuable exercise.

Below are additional ways to how you can generate ideas:

4. **Connect the Dots:** Many groundbreaking ideas come from combining two or more existing concepts in a new way. Look for connections between seemingly unrelated ideas, and explore how they can be merged to create something innovative. This is where creativity plays a crucial role.

5. **Look for Inspiration:** Inspiration can come from many sources: nature, art, other industries, or even everyday conversations. Sometimes, the best ideas come when you're not actively considering them. Keep your mind open and allow yourself to be inspired by the world around you.

6. **Test, Refine, and Repeat:** An idea remains theoretical until it is tested. Start small, test your idea in a controlled environment, and gather feedback. Use what you learn to improve, refine the idea, and repeat the cycle until you get the desired result.

Conception And Misconception Of Ideas

Just a moment ago, we looked at a simple guide on generating ideas, and I hope you're ready to implement it. As we move forward in this chapter, 'Convert the Idea to Valuable Assets,' let's explore two concepts: the conception and misconception of ideas.

A concept could be likened to an idea, a plan, or an intention, so when you generate an idea, you are generating a concept—a framework for a project. At first, it might seem sketchy or incomplete, but within it lies the potential for something far more significant, much like the blueprint of a future edifice. In its early stages, a concept is intangible; it's a thought or an abstract that cannot be physically handled. Yet, this idea or concept is the seed from which tangible assets eventually grow. It's like holding a single seed, yet in that seed lies the potential of an entire forest.

Conception, derived from the word "concept," refers to the process or formation of an idea or concept. Interestingly, this terminology is the same as the process of pregnancy. Just as a woman is said to have conceived when she becomes pregnant, so too are you "pregnant" with ideas when a concept takes root in your mind. Often, conception occurs quietly, without much fanfare, just as a woman might not immediately realise she is pregnant until she notices certain signs or missed her period. Likewise, an idea may not always announce itself spectacularly, but it holds within it the power to transform your life, moving you from debt to wealth and leading you to a place of influence and affluence.

When a woman discovers she is pregnant, the initial excitement is often palpable, with family and friends rejoicing over the newborn on the way. This mirrors the excitement that comes with the conception of a new idea. You feel a surge of joy and anticipation for what this fresh concept could bring, imagining the possibilities and potential it holds. However, just as a woman soon realises that pregnancy comes with its own challenges—morning sickness, food cravings, and physical changes—so does the journey of nurturing an idea come with its own set of demands and responsibilities.

The initial thrill of a new idea can quickly give way to the reality of the hard work required to bring it to fruition. You might find yourself needing to sacrifice sleep, step out of your comfort zone, or take on tasks you've never done before. These challenges can be daunting, but they are the necessary price to ensure that your idea grows and matures into something valuable. Just as a woman must care for herself and her unborn child during pregnancy, you must also diligently nurture your idea through all stages of its development.

The journey from the conception of a fetus to the delivery of a newborn is a challenging process. It requires the mother's effort and the support of her family, friends, doctors, nurses, and caregivers. Their combined efforts ensure that she safely brings her child into the world. Similarly, when you conceive an idea, you take on the responsibility of nurturing and developing it. But you're not alone in this process—you'll need the support of others to help you turn your idea into a valuable asset. Just as a mother's work isn't done until she delivers her baby, your journey isn't complete until your idea becomes tangible and beneficial.

However, it's essential to recognise that not all pregnancies result in the birth of a child. Miscarriages can happen, and the same is true for ideas. Many ideas are aborted before they ever have the chance to be realised. Imagine the world if every conceived idea reached its full potential. The grave is often said to be the wealthiest place on earth because of all the ideas that never saw the light of day. This is one of the key reasons why I've written this book—to ensure that you not only generate ideas but also successfully convert them into valuable assets. Don't let your ideas be among those lost to time. Guard and nurture them, and let your journey to wealth creation begin.

Just as a mother endures the intense travail of labour pains before the joy of holding her newborn, so must you endure the challenging moments of bringing your idea to life. For those who have experienced it, labour is a period of both immense pain and anticipation. Yet, when the baby is finally born, the pain is overshadowed by overwhelming joy and relief. In the same way, the darkest moments of your journey to actualising an idea can feel like labour pains—difficult, exhausting, and sometimes even overwhelming. But these moments also indicate that you're close to bringing your idea into the world. If you can endure just a little longer, you'll soon experience the joy and fulfilment of seeing your idea become a reality.

The generation of an idea is not the final destination but merely the beginning of a journey filled with work, challenges, and responsibilities. Your idea is like a seed that requires nurturing, patience, and effort to grow into something valuable. Converting your idea into a valuable asset is where the real work lies, and it is the product of this work that ultimately benefits the world, brings you fulfilment, and channels fortune your way.

Now that we've explored the concept of idea conception, it's time to consider "the misconception of ideas." Understanding this will help you avoid pitfalls that can derail even the most promising concepts and ideas.

We have seen that a concept can be likened to an idea, a plan, or an intention, so a misconception could be referred to as a wrong concept. It is an idea or concept that is incorrect or based on faulty understanding, misinformation, or flawed reasoning. Misconception could be at the level of the generation of the idea, or it could be when you are communicating your idea to another person. They may not understand what you are talking about and could misconceive your thoughts and ideas. The central thing to misconception is the lack of understanding, which calls for caution.

Much like an ectopic pregnancy, where the developing baby is positioned outside the womb, an idea that is misunderstood or built on a faulty foundation may not give the desired positive result. In such cases of an ectopic pregnancy, the expertise of a doctor is required to ensure the safety of the mother. Similarly, when an idea is based on misconception, it may take the guidance of a mentor, advisor, or expert to realign the concept and steer it back on track.

Misconceptions are not something you want to deal with, but they are sometimes unavoidable, especially when bringing a novel idea into the world.

When you share your ideas with others, it's natural for them to struggle to understand or even reject the concept entirely. This is especially true when the idea is novel, revolutionary or ahead of its time. Imagine living a century ago and hearing someone describe their plan to fly across the Atlantic Ocean or communicate via video call with someone thousands of miles away. Such ideas would have seemed odd, perhaps even impossible, and would likely have been met with scepticism or outright disbelief.

Yet, the human mind is capable of extraordinary feats, and what once seemed impossible can become commonplace in just a few years. The innovations we take for granted today were once the subject of disbelief and misunderstanding. This highlights the importance of not letting misconceptions discourage you. Instead, recognise them for what they are and be sure that you have the right foundation and understanding in the first place.

Our world is evolving, maybe rapidly evolving, and the possibilities are endless and breathtaking. It is almost certain that future innovations will likely make today's advancements seem primitive. This calls for insights and foresight—learning to see into the future without judging it by what we can see now.

Thomas Edison, the renowned inventor, once conceived the idea of the Ediphone—a device intended to record and playback voice recordings, making information transcription faster and more efficient. However, when Edison first presented the Ediphone to his sales team, they did not share his enthusiasm. Edwin Barnes, however, saw what others could not see, and he came up with plans to sell the Ediphone, which granted him a partnership with Edison.

A Simple Guide On How To Convert Your Ideas To Valuable Assets

Your ideas are only as valuable as your actions to bring them to life. They are useless until they are converted into useful products and services that can impact the world. Therefore, it is essential not to remain stagnant at the idea stage but to actively work towards transforming your concepts into valuable assets that can benefit others. This guide will walk you through the steps necessary to turn your ideas into reality.

1. **<u>Clarify and Refine Your Ideas</u>**

    Understand the core value of your idea. What problem does it intend to solve? Who will benefit from it? Determine who will benefit from your idea. Understand their needs, preferences, and pain points. The better you understand your target audience, the more effectively you can tailor your idea to meet their demands.

    You may also examine similar products or services in the market, learning from their successes and mistakes. This will help you position your idea uniquely and avoid potential pitfalls.

Make sure you can articulate the details of the idea clearly. Refine it until it comes to taste. Do not be discouraged at the first sketch because it is not likely to be perfect at the beginning, but continue to clarify and refine until it comes to taste. Also, you do not have to wait until everything is perfect before you start working on the idea. You can always refine along the way.

2. **<u>Document your ideas.</u>**

Once an idea has taken shape in your mind, the next crucial step is to document it. This involves writing down every detail of the idea, no matter how insignificant it initially seems. Documentation serves several essential purposes. It helps you organise your thoughts and see the idea more clearly, which can reveal aspects of it that you may not have initially considered. Writing down your idea also creates a record that you can refer back to, helping you track its evolution over time and your progress. The faintest ink is said to be better than the strongest memory, so documentation is crucial.

A well-documented idea could also be a communication tool when you need to share your idea with others, such as potential partners, investors, or team members. It can help prevent misconceptions and ensure everyone understands the concept clearly, reducing the risk of miscommunication as you turn your idea into a valuable asset.

3. Create a Clear Plan of Action

Set clear goals. Determine what you want to achieve and when using the SMART model. Your goals should be Specific, Measurable, Achievable, Relevant, and Time-bound. Break down the plan into smaller, manageable steps with specific deadlines. This will save you from feeling overwhelmed. Celebrate each small win along the way. Enjoy the journey because it's not just about achieving the goals that matter but also about enjoying the process and the person you become along the way.

4. Develop a Prototype or Minimum Viable Product (MVP)

Create a Minimum Viable Product (MVP) or prototype that embodies the core functionality of your idea. This will help you test the waters and get feedback before fully committing resources.

5. Test and Iterate

Share your prototype or MVP with a small group of users or stakeholders. Collect their feedback to understand what works and what needs improvement. Use the feedback to refine your idea. This might involve tweaking the design, functionality, or even the target market. Be flexible and open to change.

6. **Secure Resources and Support**

Build a Team. If your idea requires expertise beyond your own, recruit people who share your vision and can contribute to different aspects of the project. Depending on the scale of your idea, you may need financial support. Consider seeking financial support.

7. **Protect Your Idea**

If your idea is innovative, consider securing intellectual property rights such as patents, trademarks, or copyrights. This protects your idea from being copied and ensures you can fully capitalise on its value.

8. **Launch and Market Your Idea**

Develop a Marketing Strategy. Create a plan to promote your idea to your target audience.

Utilise various channels such as social media, email marketing, and content marketing to reach potential customers. Engage marketing professionals as you grow. Reach out to potential supporters and investors.

Build a Brand. Establish a strong brand identity that resonates with your audience. Create a structure, entity, and platform for your idea, which might include a business or company name, logo, and messaging templates, among other things.

9. **Monitor and Scale**

After launching, monitor the performance of your product or service. Use metrics like sales, customer feedback among others, to gauge success. If your idea proves successful, plan how to scale.

10. Reinvest and Innovate

Use the profits generated from your idea to develop further and expand your business. Stay Innovative. Continue to innovate and improve your products and services. The market constantly evolves, so staying ahead of trends and refining your ideas will help you maintain a competitive edge.

Converting your idea into a valuable asset requires a deliberate and systematic approach. Following the steps outlined in the guide above can transform your abstract concepts into tangible products or services that will benefit you and the world. Remember, the journey from idea to asset is not always straightforward, but with persistence, careful planning, and a willingness to adapt, you can turn your innovative thoughts into lasting success.

As we conclude this chapter on converting ideas into valuable assets, it's clear that the journey from conception to realisation is both challenging and rewarding. Your ideas, no matter how small, can create significant impact and wealth if nurtured and developed with care.

Now that we've explored how to turn your ideas into something valuable, it's time to consider a crucial question: What do you have that can help you on this journey? In the next chapter, Key 4: What Do You Have?, we will delve into identifying and leveraging your existing resources to further your path toward success. Come along.

KEY FOUR

What Do You Have?

You've come a long way in unlocking the keys to financial success, and your commitment to reading this far deserves recognition. Your dedication is a testament to your desire for change and growth, which is a powerful step toward achieving your financial aspirations.

In Chapter One, we explored how being a good person alone doesn't automatically credit your account with money—your goodness must be paired with sound financial principles to break free from poverty. In Chapter Two, we delved into the importance of seeking solutions rather than bailouts, and in Chapter

Three, we discussed the steps to converting your ideas into valuable assets. Moving into Chapter Four, we'll focus on something fundamental: understanding and leveraging what you already have. This chapter is about recognising the resources, skills, and networks at your disposal that you may not have noticed and leveraging them for your financial success.

Money is referred to as currency because it flows like a current in the direction of value. If you want more money, then you must be ready to offer something of value in return. When you solve people's problems or meet their needs, they willingly part with their money in exchange for the benefits you provide. This fundamental principle means that you must have something to exchange for money—whether it's a product, a service, or a skill. Money will not come your way if you have nothing to offer. This concept in wealth creation is crucial for you to understand.

Many people are frustrated about financial matters because they expect to earn money without offering anything of real value in return. They might dream of wealth but lack the resources, skills, or products others are willing to pay for. This disconnect leads to disappointment and even desperation. The truth is, you can't create wealth from nothing. You must identify what you have—your skills, knowledge, talents, or even your network—and learn how to leverage these resources effectively to create value.

Understanding this concept is crucial because it shifts your focus from what you lack to what you already possess. Instead of wishing for wealth to come your way, you start to think about the resources at your disposal and how they can be transformed into something valuable. This is an essential key to wealth creation: recognising and maximising the potential of what you already have.

If you try to obtain money without offering something of value in return, you're left with only unethical options, like stealing, robbery, scamming and crime. These are the paths people might take when they seek to gain wealth without contributing anything to the society. However, true wealth is built on the exchange of value, not on taking what doesn't belong to you. To avoid falling into this trap, it's essential to focus on what you can genuinely offer in return for the wealth you seek.

Imagine if I decided to walk into a courtroom and attempt to represent someone in a legal case, expecting to earn money for my efforts. It wouldn't take long for me to realise that this approach will fail—because I'm not trained as a lawyer. My training is in medicine, not law. Trying to earn money in a field where I have no expertise would only lead to frustration and failure.

However, what I could do instead is leverage my resources to support those who are law experts. For instance, by investing in a law firm, I could earn returns based on their expertise and hard work. This illustrates a fundamental principle: you earn money by providing something of value, whether it's your skills and services or by investing in others with the expertise you lack. The flow of money follows the flow of value; to tap into that flow, you must understand and utilise what you have.

STOP LOOKING OUTWARD, START LOOKING INWARD!

As we continue our journey toward wealth creation, it's essential to shift our focus from looking outward to looking inward. Many people spend their lives searching outward, hoping to find opportunities, wealth, or success in places far from themselves. They believe the key to their success lies in acquiring something they don't yet possess. However, the actual starting point for wealth creation lies within. The resources and potential you need are already inside you, waiting to be discovered and harnessed. In this section, we'll explore the importance of looking inward, recognising the value of what you already have, and how to use it effectively to create the wealth you desire.

If you find yourself without a job, it's easy to fall into the trap of fantasising about the perfect job you desire or worrying endlessly about the lack of one. But instead of focusing on what you don't have, it's crucial to shift your attention to what you do have. Everyone possesses something, whether a skill, talent or even an experience, that can be turned into a source of income. We often overlook these resources, taking them for granted, without realising that they are the key to solving our financial challenges.

The key is to stop looking outward for solutions and start recognising the potential in what's already in your possession. Perhaps you have a talent for cooking, a knack for fixing things, or a creative skill like writing or graphic design. Maybe you have a computer at home, a family business you can contribute to, or even valuable relationships and communication skills that could open doors for you. The list is endless. When harnessed correctly, these resources can be converted into valuable assets that generate income and set you on a path to financial stability. All you need is to see the opportunity in and around you. The solution to your financial troubles isn't far away.

So, rather than waiting for a job opportunity to come knocking, ask yourself what you have right now that can be leveraged. It might not seem like much at first, but with the right mindset and effort, even the smallest of resources can be transformed into something of great value. **The journey to wealth often begins small. Do not be ashamed to start little.**

There was once a woman who worked in an establishment but suddenly found herself retrenched from her job. She was devastated, confused, and overwhelmed by the uncertainty of her financial future, especially since she had no savings. Desperate for guidance, she sought out the advice of Myles Munroe. Instead of offering immediate sympathy, he asked her a simple question, "What do you have at home?"

Myles Munroe often taught that sometimes losing a job is a sign that it's time to start your work—what you were born to do. Perhaps it was time for the woman to discover her potential instead of working for someone else. The woman, still bewildered, replied that she had an oven at home. Myles Munroe then advised her to take her last paycheck, pay her tithe, and use the remainder to bake cookies. He told her to take the cookies to where she had been fired and give them away for free. The woman was shocked—how could giving away her last resources possibly help her survive? Despite her doubts, she decided to follow his advice.

She bought the ingredients, baked the cookies, and delivered them. To her surprise, the next day, they contacted her asking for more cookies, but this time, she requested payment. They paid her in advance, and she fulfilled the order. This small act of faith, obedience, and leveraging her gift led to the birth of her own cookie business. Over time, her business grew, and she became an employer instead of an employee. One day, she met Myles Munroe again. She handed him a beautifully packaged cookie and a $10,000 gift— a testament to how dramatically her life has changed because she looked inward and harnessed her hidden potential.

This story illustrates the power of looking inward and using what you already have, no matter how small it might seem. It reminds us that within each of us lies the potential to transform our circumstances if we're willing to recognise and act on them.

As we continue our discussion, let us reconsider the story of the poor widow and Elisha, the prophet. The widow approached Elisha, likely hoping for a financial bailout from the community of prophets. She might have thought that her debt could be cleared if everyone contributed a little. However, Elisha's response was different from what she expected. Instead of offering her money, he asked, "What can I do to help you? Tell me, what do you have in the house?" She replied, "Nothing at all, except a flask of olive oil."[1]

This response reveals a common mindset: undervaluing what we already possess. The widow thought her little oil was insignificant, but it held the key to her financial breakthrough. She was poor but not without resources. That small flask of oil, which she had overlooked, was the solution to her financial problems. Had she and her husband recognised its potential earlier, they might never have fallen into debt in the first place. Perhaps her husband's life could have been different if they had understood the value of what they had.

The question Elisha asked the widow is what I am asking you today: "What do you have?" *Often, we focus so much on what we lack that we fail to see the value in what we already possess.* Whether it's a skill, a small amount of savings, a connection, or even just an idea, there's something within your reach that can be transformed into a valuable asset. It's time to stop underestimating what you have and start exploring how it can be used to solve your problems and create wealth.

Now that you've grasped the importance of recognising the potential and resources you already possess, it's time to take action. I encourage you to pause for a moment, grab a notepad and a pen, and write down 20 things you have right now that could be transformed into valuable assets. At first, the ideas may come quickly—perhaps you'll think of a skill you've mastered or a piece of equipment you own. But as you get further down the list, it might become more challenging. That's perfectly normal. Push yourself to complete the list because the most overlooked and undervalued resources often have the most tremendous potential.

Once you've completed your list, take each item and think about how it could be converted into something of value. Could a hobby be turned into a side business? Could a connection or relationship open doors to new opportunities? Write down these possibilities, no matter how small or insignificant they may seem. After brainstorming, please choose one or two ideas that resonate with you the most and start developing a plan to bring them to life. This exercise is about identifying what you have and unlocking the hidden potential within those resources to generate income and create wealth. You might want to refer to the previous chapter on "Convert the Idea to Valuable Assets" for further clarity on how to convert an idea to valuable assets.

If you do this exercise well, you'll likely discover that you have more opportunities at your disposal than you initially realised. As someone said, ***"You can be jobless, but you cannot be workless."*** Remember that you earn money with what you have because money flows in the direction of value. The journey may not be easy, but the rewards are worthwhile.

I recently heard a business tycoon share a remarkable story that underscores the importance of recognising and acting on what you have. This man, who graduated from the university in 1972, and some years after graduating, was living the life many dreamt of—he had a great job, a well-furnished apartment, a new car, and cleaners attending to his needs at home and work. He was also leading a team at his workplace. Life was seemingly perfect, but then he felt a strong inner prompting to leave his secure job and start his own business. It was a difficult decision, but he couldn't ignore the call.

When he handed in his resignation, his boss was shocked and thought he had lost his mind. His boss even told him he would hold onto the resignation letter for a few days to give him a chance to reconsider. But his decision was final. He left his job and started his business in a one-room office, where he was the only employee. This was far from the life he was accustomed to. He would arrive at his new office early, lock the door behind himself, and clean the place by himself—a humbling experience compared to his previous lifestyle.

As he began his entrepreneurial journey, he recalled a childhood memory of helping his grandmother produce palm oil on the farm. The process was manual, labour-intensive, and inefficient, as they could only extract a small percentage of the oil from the palm fruits. This childhood experience had always made him wonder if there was a way to speed up the process and extract a more significant percentage of the oil more efficiently. He could have let go of the thought, but it turned out to be his own "flask of oil," much like the poor widow in the biblical story.

He decided to act on this idea, and that decision changed the course of his life. What started as a childhood fantasy became the foundation of his business. Today, he is a successful businessman with a network of companies and is a major player in the palm oil industry in Nigeria and West Africa. His journey began with a simple idea from his past, something he already had, and by recognising its potential, he built a thriving business empire worth millions.

Don't expect money to rain down from the sky when you pray for financial solutions. Instead, focus your prayers and reflections to seek answers to questions like, "What do I have that can launch me from debt to wealth? What skills or assets can I leverage to create a steady cash flow?" Recognise that you are not without resources; we are born with unique abilities, talents, connections, and communities that we can tap into. All you need to do is identify these resources and unlock their potential. **Stop Looking Outward, Start Looking Inward!**

Before we conclude our discussion in this chapter, let's consider the story of Hagar and Ishmael. They carried a bottle of water as they travelled into the wilderness. When the water ran out, Hagar became desperate, unable to see any way to find more. In her despair, she left her son under the shade of a bush and walked a distance away, saying, "I don't want to watch the boy die."⁵ She had lost all hope, prepared to face death in her lack. Both Hagar and her son cried, and while God heard their cries, Ishmael's cry moved Him to respond, not that of the mother. Why?. "But God heard the boy crying, and the angel of God called to Hagar from heaven, "Hagar, what's wrong? Do not be afraid! God has heard the boy crying as he lies there.""⁵

It was almost as if God was surprised that she was crying, knowing that the very thing she was crying for was already within her reach. The story continues, "Then God opened Hagar's eyes, and she saw a well full of water. She quickly filled her water container and gave the boy a drink."⁵ The well had been there all along—the solution to her lack was right before her, but she did not see it. The abundance she needed was within her reach; she simply lacked the insight to recognise it. May you receive the insight to see your own 'flask of oil' and your 'well'—the hidden resources and opportunities already in and around you.

As we conclude this chapter, it's essential to remember wealth creation involves recognising and valuing what you already possess. Whether it's a skill, a talent, a relationship, a childhood dream, or an experience, what you have right now holds the potential to transform your financial situation. The key is to stop looking outward for solutions and start looking inward at the resources you already have. Once you do this, you'll see that you are far from empty-handed, as the seed to your future prosperity is already in your hands.

It is time to consider the next key: What You Have is Enough—Grow It!

See you in the next chapter.

KEY FIVE

What You Have Is Enough—Grow It!

Congratulations on making it this far in your journey! Often, we are tempted to believe that our resources are too small, our skills too basic, or our connections too few. But the truth is, everything great started small. It's time to shift your mindset from one of scarcity to one of growth, where you begin to nurture what you have and watch it expand into greater opportunities and wealth- What You Have is Enough—Grow It!

Many people remain in poverty, not because they lack the resources, but because they fail to recognise the

value of what they already possess. It's a common misconception that wealth comes from acquiring something new and outside of ourselves. However, the resources for breaking free from poverty are often already within our reach. The challenge lies in identifying and growing them.

Consider the story of the widow and her small flask of oil, which we've discussed before. She might have laughed in disbelief if someone had told her that the little oil she had left was the solution to all her financial woes. To her, it was just a tiny flask of oil, nothing special, certainly not enough to pay off her debts or secure her future. And yet, that very flask of oil held the potential to transform her life.

This oil, small and seemingly insignificant, was with her all along—even before her husband passed away. The value is always there, waiting to be unlocked. The lesson here is profound: what you have, no matter how small it may seem, has the potential to multiply and grow, just like a seed. A single seed may look tiny, but within it lies the potential for a forest. Similarly, the skills, resources, or ideas you possess, no matter how modest, hold the potential for great expansion if you only recognise their worth and commit to growing them.

IDENTIFY YOUR SEED!

A seed, in its simplest form, is the starting point of something magnificent. Just as a mighty oak tree emerges from a tiny acorn, the inherent gift and talent, ideas, skills, or resources you possess—no matter how small they seem—have the potential to grow into something powerful and transformative. *"The creation of a thousand forests is in one acorn,"* said Ralph Waldo Emerson, reminding us that within each seed lies the potential for something extraordinary. A seed might look ordinary, but in it is the 'extraordinary'; therefore, identify your seed and grow it.

As I was reflecting on the idea of identifying your seed, a verse came to my mind where God commands the human race to be fruitful: "Then God blessed them, and God said to them, 'Be fruitful and multiply; fill the earth and subdue it; have dominion over the fish of the sea, over the birds of the air, and over every living thing that moves on the earth.'"[6] This wasn't a suggestion; it was a command—a clear directive that is crucial for anyone seeking a life of fulfilment and prosperity. The command begins with "be fruitful," which is particularly interesting. God didn't say "be seedful" because providing the seed was His responsibility. Your role is to turn that seed into fruit, to multiply what you have been given. You are full of seeds already. No one is without a seed. What you need to do is to identify the seeds and turn them into fruit. It is simple, right? As simple as it may sound, many find it difficult to follow this instruction. Countless people have gone to their graves without ever identifying their seeds, let alone turning them into fruits. Unsurprisingly, the grave is often said to be the wealthiest place on earth—full of unwritten books, unsung songs, unbuilt companies, unfounded schools, undiscovered innovations, and so on.

Turning your seed into fruit is where the real work lies. If you've ever farmed or worked alongside a farmer, you'll know that transforming a seed into a fruit requires a great deal of effort, time, and dedication. The time it takes for a seed to grow into a fruit-bearing plant varies depending on the type of seed and the kind of fruit it will produce. For instance, a maize seed might take about four months to yield its harvest, while an orange seed might take years to grow into a fruit-bearing tree. However, once the orange tree is established, it produces fruit year after year, unlike the maize plant, which has a shorter lifecycle. Can you see the difference?

The work involved in turning a seed into fruit starts with preparing the soil. This includes clearing the land, ploughing it, and planting the seed. After planting, the seed requires regular watering; sometimes, you may need to provide a shed before transplanting it to its permanent location. Even then, your work isn't done. You must clear the weeds, nurture the plant, and protect it from pests and rodents until it matures. This process mirrors the effort required to convert your inherent gifts, potential, and talents into valuable assets. It's not a one-time task but a continuous commitment to nurturing your seed until it bears fruit, and then you work to protect and multiply the fruits. The work required to turn your seed into fruit differs from that needed to multiply the fruit. I hope you get that. Let us go through the Creator's instruction again: "Then God blessed them, and God said to them, 'Be fruitful and multiply; fill the earth and subdue it; have dominion over the fish of the sea, over the birds of the air, and over every living thing that moves on the earth.'"[6]

The time and effort you invest in cultivating your seed may span weeks, months, or even years before you see the first sign of success. But once your seed starts to bear fruit, it becomes a continuous source of sustenance and prosperity. The journey may be long and challenging, but the rewards are enduring. When you invest in your gifts and talents, you set yourself up for a lifetime of returns.

Do Not Be Quick To Forget That You Are A Steward

We quickly forget our responsibility as stewards, and to make it worse, we do not even remember that we are stewards in the first place. How can we act as we ought to if we do not know ourselves or our roles? It is akin to the story of a lion taken as a cub by a hunter and raised among sheep. Though the lion grew strong, it never saw itself as a lion but as a sheep and behaved accordingly. This highlights the concept of identity. Do not forget that you were not a result of chance but of intentionality in the mind of God, and His purpose was for you to be a steward and manager.

Who is a steward? A steward can be referred to as a resource manager, someone entrusted to care for a property or an individual entrusted with resources saddled with the responsibility to keep, invest, and multiply them.

The Creator is a businessman; like any businessman, He desires to increase and profit. When He created the birds, He clearly instructed them: ***"Be fruitful and multiply."***[6] This directive wasn't exclusive to the birds; it extended to other animals, sea creatures, plants, and, most importantly, mankind. He explicitly instructed humans to be fruitful, multiply, replenish, subdue, and have dominion over the earth. This is a call to take the role of a businessman and a call to stewardship and responsibility.

When you fail to turn your gifts into fruits, you are not following the instructions the Creator gave you because He said, "Be fruitful." Your gifts can be likened to seeds that need to be planted, nurtured, and cultivated into fruits that benefit you and others. It's no coincidence that God didn't start the instruction by saying, "Be seedful." He has already provided the seeds—the resources you need to be fruitful. He has called you to steward these resources for profit and increase.

There are steps and processes involved in a seed becoming a fruit. A farmer understands this well; they prepare the soil before planting the seed, ensuring it is suitable for growth. If the soil isn't conducive, the seed may not germinate or could wither soon after sprouting. The story of the Sower illustrates this vividly: some seeds fell on the roadside and were eaten by birds, some on rocky ground and sprouted but withered due to lack of proper roots, others among thorns were choked, but those on fertile soil yielded abundant increase. Even among the seeds that fell on good soil, some multiplied by thirty, some by sixty, and some by a hundred. Soil preparation is crucial for seed growth.

You need to provide the right environment for your seed's growth. Don't let negative thoughts or distractions like social media and movies choke your gift. Your mind is the soil for your seed; prepare it well.

It's no wonder Solomon, in his wisdom, advised, "Guard your heart with all diligence, for out of it spring the issues of life."[7]

This is just one step in turning your seed into fruit. If this is just a step, you could see that turning your seed or gift into fruit or finished products requires diligence and commitment. Besides preparing the soil, you must plant the seed, nurture it, protect it from weeds, pests, and insects, and then wait patiently. Many seek shortcuts, wanting instant results, but growing your gifts to fruition takes patience, perseverance, and consistency—that's your work.

The story of the grass and the bamboo is a powerful illustration of patience, consistency, and their eventual rewards. When you plant grass seeds, it sprouts within a week or so. It grows quickly, reaching its full height in a matter of weeks. However, once it peaks, it remains relatively unchanged and withers quickly. On the other hand, when you plant bamboo seeds, you water and nurture them, but nothing seems to happen for the first year or even the second, third and fourth year. It requires consistent care and attention without any visible signs of progress.

Yet, in the fifth year, something remarkable occurs. The bamboo shoots begin to emerge, and within just a few weeks, they can grow up to 80 feet tall. This sudden growth isn't because the bamboo suddenly grew fast; it's because it spent the first few years establishing a robust underground root system. This story teaches that your efforts may not yield immediate results like the bamboo. You may need to patiently nurture your skills, gifts, relationships, or endeavours without seeing visible progress. But if you remain consistent and steadfast in your efforts, the rewards will eventually manifest, often in ways beyond your imagination. Just as the bamboo's growth astonishes those who witness it, your perseverance and dedication will lead to extraordinary outcomes.

Remember, people are attracted to your fruit, not your seed. They are interested in what they would gain from you. When Jesus walked the earth, people were all over him, not out of love for Him but because they desired the benefits He offered. They travelled far and endured hardships, even travelling through the night to obtain the fruit of His ministry.

Ultimately, people will pay you for what they can gain from you—your fruit. So, be fruitful.

Before concluding that you haven't been given anything to manage or care for, consider the resources the Creator has entrusted you for stewardship. It's up to you to convert these resources into valuable fruits-products and services. What are the resources He has given you to profit?

Here are some of the resources God has given you to nurture and profit from:

1. **Your time:** He has given you time on Earth. This resource is distributed equally to everyone, regardless of age, gender, or status. Each one of us has twenty-four hours a day to invest.

Unfortunately, many squander this precious resource on unproductive activities. Some liken time to money, a comparison with some truth, as time is not just money but life itself. Every moment spent, whether watching a movie or engaging in meaningful endeavours like writing a book, is engaging in a transaction which could be a good or bad investment. When you watch a free movie or scroll through pages on the internet for free, it's not free because you paid for it - you paid with your time. Time is a form of currency. By reading this book, for instance, you are investing your time in gaining valuable information and engaging in a productive pursuit and investment which would yield dividends. The next time you engage in an activity, ask yourself if it is worth the time you are paying for it. If it does, continue with the activity; if it does not, you know what to do.

2. **Your mind:** Your mind is among the most potent resources given to you by the Creator. The mind determines your trajectory in life, shaping who you become and what you achieve. Therefore, it is essential to pay close attention to this resource and capitalising on its potential. I am writing a book on harnessing the power of the mind, which I regard as the richest mine on Earth. You may want to read the book when it is ready.

3. **Your attention.** This is equally crucial. Consider that everyone vies for your attention. Its sought-after nature signifies its value. Advertisements, social media content, salespersons, and marketers all compete for your attention, while you may not even realise the significance of this resource. You must know how to focus your attention on productive work and activity.

4. **Your relationships.** This is another resource you need to nurture, which is crucial to your growth and success. We do not live in isolation. You need people—like-minded individuals and those who have gone beyond you—to help you unleash your gifts upon the world. Your immediate family should also be prioritised as you journey toward profiting with your gift.

5. **Your unique abilities and gifts.** There are no two people on Earth who are the same, not even identical twins; they have traits that differentiate them. I believe that's why we all have unique fingerprints, showing that we possess exceptional abilities and gifts that can benefit the world. No one else can offer the world what you have in the same way you can, so it's crucial to identify your unique abilities and gifts and use them to make the world a better place. You are called to steward these unique abilities and gifts. What would you do

with them? Would you profit and bless the world with them, hide them, or abuse them?

It is also crucial that I emphasise that God is a businessman. Many people do not align with this concept of the Creator. They are willing to go to heaven as an escape plan without considering that this isn't the primary reason they are on Earth - they have got to profit the kingdom they long to go to.

Imagine you are a businessman and you invested in a business, say a million dollars. You asked a manager to manage the money and any other resources you have put into building the business into a profitable company. What do you expect from the manager? Of course, you expect the manager to increase the returns on investment. When you request an annual return or find out how the business has done for the past year, you realise that the manager has done nothing. How would you feel? And what would you do? Or, to make it worse, the one million dollars you invested in the business has been depleted to one hundred thousand dollars. What would be your response to this?

This demonstrates what many individuals are doing. The Creator has invested millions of dollars worth of resources in them, but they do not profit from the investment. Do you think the Creator wouldn't ask about how you managed His investment when you show up to Him?

There is a story that illustrates the Creator, where He gave His servants money to do business until He returned. 'So he called ten of his servants, delivered to them ten minas, and said to them, "Do business till I come."' I love how the New International Version puts it: 'So he called ten of his servants and gave them ten minas. "Put this money to work," he said, "until I come back."'[8] You have got to put your gifts to work.

It Is Your Duty To Identify Your Seed

Do you know that the responsibility of identifying your seed lies with you? No one else can do it for you.

While a mentor or someone close to you might help point out your potential or gifts, the ultimate responsibility to recognise and embrace your seed is yours. Your seed is uniquely yours, embedded within you by design, and it's not hidden in some far-off place where you have to search endlessly. In His wisdom, God has placed your seed so close to you that you won't miss it if you are not distracted.

Your seed will often be evident to you because it resonates with your deepest interests, talents, and passions. It comes naturally to you, something you find yourself drawn to repeatedly. The challenge is not in finding your seed but in recognising it amid the distractions of life. If you take the time to reflect and pay attention, you will identify your seed, and when you do, you will know what to do with it. If I may ask, "From what you have learned so far, what are you supposed to do with your seed?"

IDEAS BUILD UPON ONE ANOTHER

Every great enterprise starts with a single idea, often small and seemingly insignificant. It is like a seed that, when nurtured and developed, grows into something far more substantial than initially imagined. Many successful businesses began this way — what started as a simple thought or observation evolved into a thriving venture. The key lies in recognising the potential within that initial idea and being willing to act on it, even when it appears modest.

Consider how a single idea can spark a series of developments. When you nurture and build upon your ideas, they have the potential to evolve into something much greater than their original form. The most successful people and companies often started with a small concept but did not stop there. They continued to innovate, adapt, and expand on their original ideas, allowing them to flourish into something remarkable. The power of an idea lies not just in its initial conception but in its continuous growth and the opportunities it creates along the way.

Ideas build upon one another. If you don't act on the first idea, the subsequent ones won't surface. This is how many of the great businesses around us today were established. It all began with a single idea, and as that idea grew, it sparked the development of additional, complementary ideas, creating a cascading effect. So, remember: **What you have is enough—just be sure to grow it!**

As we conclude this chapter, it's clear that what you have is more than enough—it's the foundation for your success. The seeds of greatness are already within you, waiting to be nurtured and grown. The journey of transforming what you have into something extraordinary is challenging, but it's also greatly rewarding. Remember, every great business, every remarkable achievement, began with someone recognising and cultivating a small idea.

But having an idea and identifying your seed is only the beginning. The next crucial step is action. In the next chapter, "Key 6: Nothing Happens If You Do Not Act," we will explore the importance of taking deliberate, consistent steps toward your goals. Get ready to discover how action is the bridge between where you are and where you want to be. You won't want to miss it!

Key Six

Nothing Happens If You Do Not Act

You've come a long way in this journey, and I want to take a moment to applaud your commitment. Reading this far is no small feat, and it shows that you're serious about transforming your life and unlocking the keys to wealth. But let me tell you something crucial—no matter how much knowledge you gain, nothing will change unless you act on it. You could have the best ideas and the most detailed plans, but without action, all of that will remain just potential. In this chapter, we will dive into why action is the catalyst that turns dreams into reality and how you can start taking meaningful steps today. Let us get started.

The story of the poor widow and the prophet Elisha is a reminder that nothing happens without action. The widow found herself in a desperate situation, but her willingness to act on the prophet's instructions turned her situation around. She didn't just listen; she acted. She gathered jars, poured her small amount of oil, and witnessed a miracle of multiplication. Her story would have remained one of poverty and despair if she hadn't taken that first step of faith. It was her action that changed her story for the better.

Nothing happens if you do not act. It's not enough to dream about your ideas or envision a better life; you must take concrete steps to make those dreams a reality. Conceiving an idea is just the beginning—a signal that you have work to do. Ideas are like seeds, but unless you plant and nurture them, they will remain as seeds and never grow into the trees they're meant to be. Sitting idly, hoping for things to change on their own, is a sure path to frustration and missed opportunities.

So, don't let laziness or fear hold you back. Get to work! The world is full of people with great ideas, but the ones who succeed are those who take action. Your ideas are your roadmap, but your actions will get you to your destination. Start today, and you'll be amazed at the transformation that can happen when you move from thinking to doing. As Brain Tracy would say, ***"If you want to change your future, take action and take action now."***

Your ideas, no matter how brilliant or innovative, are useless unless you act on them. They will remain mere thoughts and intangible if you do not take the steps necessary to bring them to life. This is why it's crucial to document your ideas and convert them into valuable assets. For further insight, kindly check the chapter on converting your ideas into valuable assets.

Writing down your ideas is essential in transforming them into tangible products. But documenting alone isn't enough; you must plan how to achieve these ideas. Break them down into actionable steps and set timelines for each. A well-laid plan is crucial.

Between the conception and actualisation of an idea is a journey. Many people do not like to walk this journey because it is often a long, winding road filled with challenges and unexpected turns. It requires effort, determination, and perseverance. There will be days when the road feels too tough, and the goals seem too far away. However, this journey, though difficult at times, has the power to transform you, and that is the beauty. It's not just about reaching the end goal; it's about the growth you experience along the way. Each step you take and each challenge you overcome shapes you into a more resilient, capable, kind, strong, emotionally intelligent, confident, and insightful person. So, don't shy away from the work required to bring your ideas to life. Embrace the journey, knowing that it's not just about what you achieve but about who you become in the process.

Before we move on, let us consider the concept of work in relation to transforming your seed into valuable assets.

WORK IS A BLESSING

In this section, we will redefine our perspective with work. Contrary to popular belief, work is not a necessary evil—it is a blessing, a pathway to fulfilment, and a path to profound meaning in your live.

The concept of work has long been intertwined with notions of struggle. From the biblical narrative of Adam and Eve's expulsion from the Garden of Eden to modern-day tales of the daily grind, we've been conditioned to view work through a lens of hardship and toil. It's no news that God cursed man because he sinned, and it was stated that he will eat out of his struggle: 'Cursed is the ground for your sake; In toil, you shall eat of it all the days of your life.'[9] But what if we challenged this narrative? What if we dared to see work not as a curse but as a gift and blessing—an opportunity to express our talents, reveal ourselves and gifts, contribute to the world, and cultivate a sense of purpose?

The Origin of Work

Let's delve into the origin of work, a narrative often overshadowed by tales of punishment and toil. We typically perceive work as stemming from man's failure to obey God. "If Adam and Eve had not sinned, I would have been enjoying myself, eating and drinking in Eden," I used to think as a young boy. This sentiment is shared by many. We wish they had not disobeyed God so that we could sleep as long as we wanted and eat anything we desired without having to work. We regard work as a consequence of their disobedience and a punishment for their transgression against the Divine. However, what if I told you that work existed before humanity disobeyed the Divine?

From the very beginning, we witness the Creator facing a chaotic earth and undertaking the task of bringing order out of the chaos. The creation story reflects the Creator at work, as it took Him six days to establish order from the earth's disorder. God worked diligently for six days, necessitating a rest on the seventh. Without such hard work, there would be no need for rest. And this occurred long before man and his disobedient act.

According to the creation story, God spoke, and those things He called into existence came into being. However, upon closer inspection, we observe that it took an entire day for some of the things He called to come into being. "God called the light Day, and the darkness He called Night. So the evening and the morning were the first day"[10]. If it were merely about speaking, it might not entail much work, but ensuring that what was spoken came into existence required a full day—a significant twenty-four hours. This process continued for six more days. This is undeniably work.

Upon completing His work, there was a sense of fulfilment and satisfaction. "Then God saw everything that He had made, and indeed it was very good. So the evening and the morning were the sixth day."[11] This also demonstrates that work is not a curse but a blessing—a path to impact, fulfilment, and worthy compensation. Work gives your thoughts an expression. It allows you to bring your thoughts and ideas to life, as seen in the creation story.

Man Was Created Because There Was Work For Him To Do

It is interesting to know that the creation of man was not merely an afterthought or a random occurrence but an outcome of purpose. The Divine does not embark on an endeavour without a reason or purpose in mind. Everything created, from the sun to the moon, serves a distinct purpose, and man is no exception. When He made the sun, He had it in mind for it to reign during the day by providing light, and when He created the moon, there was no exception in giving it a clear reason for its existence. The same applied to every other creation, including man.

When God was about to create man, there was an innovative meeting on what the man would do and the resources needed to get his assignment done. In fact, he is the brilliance of God's creative ability as he is an outcome of the greatest innovation ever. One of the exciting reasons for his creation was to engage in meaningful work, as until the time he was created, it was clearly stated that there was no man to work in the garden. "Before any plant of the field was in the earth and before any herb of the field had grown. For the Lord God had not caused it to rain on the earth, and there was no man to till the ground; ... Then the Lord God took the man and put him in the garden of Eden to tend and keep it."[12] This is far from the likely notion that he was placed in the garden for leisure without engaging in any work. He was not there to eat anything he liked, sleep as long as he could, and then eat again, but he was placed in the garden to take care of it. He was saddled with the responsibility of ensuring the smooth operation of the garden and earth. Essentially, he was called to be a manager. Perhaps the words 'manager' and 'management' are derived from the word 'man' – ***man**ager*, ***man**agement*.

We can see that work emerges not as a consequence of sin but as an intrinsic part of the creation of the human race. The first human was entrusted with the stewardship of Eden and the Earth, given the noble task of tending to its beauty and abundance. Far from being a burden, this was a call to responsibility and an invitation to co-create with God. Thus, man's purpose from the outset was not merely to indulge in idleness but to actively participate in the stewardship of creation. He wasn't there simply to satisfy his desires but to contribute to the garden's flourishing entrusted to his care.

Furthermore, it's crucial to recognise that man was created in the image and likeness of God. It was stated that 'God said, "Let Us make man in Our image, according to Our likeness; let them have dominion over the fish of the sea, over the birds of the air, and over the cattle, over all the earth and over every creeping thing that creeps on the earth.'[13] This means that man was designed to reflect the Creator, who Himself engaged in the act of creation. The Creator's work was so demanding that He rested on the seventh day. Therefore, if man was made in the likeness of God, he must also be a creator, and creation necessitates work. *There is no meaningful creation without work.*

Work serves as the vessel for expressing our creative abilities. While one can conceive endless possibilities in the mind, it is through work that these dreams manifest into tangible realities. Without the necessary effort, creations remain intangible and are devoid of any benefit. Thus, work not only unleashes the brilliance of our creative potential but also guides us towards impact, fulfilment, and compensation.

Have you ever wondered why engaging in the right work brings a sense of fulfilment? It's because *work*

provides an avenue for self-expression. Imagine living without the ability to express your innate talents—it would be like a bird grounded from flight or, a fish unable to swim or the sun unable to shine. By engaging our creative abilities and revealing our gifts and selves through meaningful work, we attain inner peace, tranquillity, and a profound sense of fulfilment of purpose. You can see that at the centre of man's existence is work to express the reason for his creation and existence.

Perhaps you're pondering on what work you are wired to do. Could it be accounting, law, medicine, or another field altogether? It could be, and it may not. I hope that is not an ambiguous answer. Here is the acid test: if your profession fails to provide uniqueness, fulfilment and an avenue for impacting others, whether you're a doctor, lawyer, or police officer, then it may simply be a job—a means of earning a living.

However, it's entirely feasible to transform your profession into more than just a source of income. You can infuse it with purpose, allowing your innate abilities and gifts to shine. Consider a teacher who not only imparts knowledge but also uplifts the downtrodden or less privileged, recognising the untapped potential in their students and guiding them toward brilliance. Or envision an artist pouring their heart into a masterpiece, creating a timeless symbol of significance. The key lesson here is to harmonise your innate gifts with your chosen profession, thereby leaving a lasting impact on the world. Doing so unlocks the path to both fulfilment and worthy compensation.

Let us consider one more thing before we conclude our discussion in this section. As a young boy, I have often wondered why Paul said, "Just as He chose us in Him before the foundation of the world."[14] I couldn't fathom how God could have chosen us before the world's creation. Did that imply we existed before the creation of the earth? Where were we if we indeed existed before God formed the earth? It wasn't until I grasped the concept of 'The two Creation' that I understood what he meant.

What is this concept all about? In his book, *"The 7 Habits of Highly Effective People,"* Stephen Covey introduces the idea of mental and physical creations. This principle illustrates that all things are created twice—first in the mind and then in the physical realm. Just as a building follows a blueprint, our physical manifestations are preceded by mental conceptions. Covey emphasises the importance of beginning with the end in mind, utilising the power of imagination to envision what we desire before bringing it into existence.

Consider, for instance, the story of an aspiring entrepreneur. Before launching a new business venture, they engage in brainstorming, strategic planning, and visualisation exercises. Through this mental creation process, they clarify their goals, identify potential obstacles, and map out actionable steps toward success. Only after solidifying their vision in their mind do they proceed to the physical creation phase—drafting business plans, securing funding, and bringing their ideas to fruition.

Similarly, let's examine an artist's journey preparing to paint a masterpiece. Before touching brush to canvas, they spend time immersed in creative contemplation, envisioning the colours, shapes, and emotions they wish to convey. Through this mental creation process, they tap into their imagination, allowing their inner vision to guide their artistic expression. They translate their mental concept into physical form only after refining their mental concept, bringing their painting to life stroke by stroke.

In both examples, the power of the two creations is evident. Individuals harness the transformative potential of imagination, clarity, and intentionality by first engaging in mental creation. This process enables them to align their actions with their desires and aspirations, paving the way for greater fulfilment and success. As Covey suggests, by beginning with the end in mind, individuals can take proactive control of their lives, shaping their destiny and manifesting their dreams into reality.

As seen above, God envisioned man on earth before creating the physical world. This was why Paul claimed that He had chosen us before the foundation of the world. In fact, it was because He had us in mind and knew what He wanted us to do—to dominate on earth—that He went all the way to create the earth. If we had not come to God's mind, there would have been no reason for forming the earth and all that is in it. In other words, we gave the earth meaning, purpose and significance.

As we draw the curtain on our discussion in this section, it is evident that work, far from being a curse, is a blessing the Creator bestowed upon humanity. From the beginning of creation, man was designed to engage in meaningful work, reflecting the image and likeness of the Creator. Through the concept of the two creations—mental and physical—we recognise that work serves as a vehicle for expressing our creative potential and fulfilling our purpose on earth. As we continue our journey, let us carry with us the understanding that *work is not a necessary evil but an opportunity to express our innate gifts and uniqueness,* thus unlocking the path to impact, fulfilment, and worthy compensation.

To further explore the concept of "work and job," I encourage you to read my book, **"FIND YOUR WORK: Unlocking Your Path to Impact, Fulfilment and Worthy Compensation."** In it, I delve into how to discover the work that truly matters, align it with your life's purpose, and find fulfilment in what you do every day. Check https://pnuxelconsulting.com/fyw or visit any of your favourite bookstores.

Though jobs may be scarce, the opportunities for meaningful work are abundant. Someone said, "You may be jobless, but you cannot be workless." Work is not about earning a paycheck; it's about fulfilling a purpose and contributing to the world around you.

You tap into a divine rhythm when you find your work—the thing you were born to do.

As we wrap up this chapter, remember that ideas alone won't change your life—action will. The journey from conception to realisation is where transformation happens. Every step you take toward actualising your ideas brings you closer to your goals and shapes you into a stronger, more resilient person. The work you put in now will yield fruits that last a lifetime, so don't hesitate—act on your ideas and watch your life change.

But the journey doesn't end here. As you take action and move closer to your goals, you'll find that you can't do it all alone. That's why the next chapter, Key 7: Cherish Your Networks and Relationships, is crucial. Your connections can open doors, provide support, and bring new opportunities. In the next chapter, we'll explore how to build, nurture, and leverage these relationships to propel you even further on your path to success. Get ready to discover the power of the people in your life!

KEY SEVEN

Cherish Your Networks And Relationships

Now, it's time to explore another important key in your journey to wealth creation — cherish your networks and relationships. Just as a seed needs soil, water, and sunlight to grow, your journey requires connections that can nurture, support, and open doors for you. In this chapter, we'll delve into how cherishing and cultivating your networks and relationships can be a powerful key to unlocking opportunities, growth, and success.

In the story we've been exploring, it might seem that the poor widow's only asset was her small flask of oil.

However, she had something else which was equally very valuable—her network of friends and neighbours. When she told the prophet what she had, he instructed her to "Borrow as many empty jars as you can from your friends and neighbours."[1] This instruction highlights the crucial role that relationships play in our lives. There's a saying that "your network is your net worth," emphasising how vital relationships are to our success. In the widow's case, her relationships were instrumental to her financial breakthrough.

Imagine if the widow had no friends or neighbours to turn to. Where would she have found the empty jars to multiply her oil? Those empty jars represented her seed capital—the resources required to start her business. She secured that seed capital from her network at a zero interest rate. This teaches us that our relationships are assets that should be nurtured. Cherish your network, as it is an invaluable asset that can open doors and provide support in ways that money simply cannot.

Also, imagine if the widow had been hostile towards her friends and neighbours. Would she have been able to borrow those jars? It's unlikely. Even if she dared to ask, her neighbours might have refused if she had not nurtured those relationships. This underscores the importance of cherishing and maintaining positive relationships. It's vital to avoid sowing seeds of bitterness in the relationships around you. Even if a relationship doesn't align with your goals or interests, it's wise to exit gracefully without causing resentment or harm.

It's also important to understand that relationships are diverse and serve different purposes. The bond between a husband and wife is inherently different from that between coworkers or neighbours. Regardless of the type, every relationship deserves respect, and it's essential to seek the good of others in your network. Avoid thinking only about what you can gain from a relationship without offering anything in return. Selfishness can damage even the strongest bonds. Instead, aim to contribute positively to those around you.

Doing good to others creates a sense of indebtedness, almost like you're depositing goodwill into the friendship and relationship account. This account can be drawn upon in times of need, even if you don't explicitly ask for it. Often, people are more than willing to go the extra mile for someone who has consistently shown kindness and support to them. This principle aligns with the universal law of sowing and reaping — you will eventually harvest what you invest in your relationships. Therefore, it's crucial to invest in your networks and relationships, no matter how small the effort might seem. Start somewhere and be consistent in your efforts.

Human nature tends to lean toward self-centeredness, focusing primarily on personal gain. However, you can choose to be intentional about putting others first. Consider how you can alleviate the struggles or pain of those in your network. Don't be a parasite that only takes from others without contributing. Instead, bring something valuable to the table. It doesn't always have to be material; offering a listening ear, giving encouragement, or helping someone with a task can be just as valuable as any tangible gift.

I once read in a book that you should always bring something when you visit someone, no matter how small. The author emphasised that it's not just about monetary gifts—there are countless ways to show you care. A simple gesture like picking a flower, writing a note of encouragement, or bringing a single piece of fruit can go a long way to show that you care. These small acts of kindness nurture your relationships and strengthen your network. As social beings, we are naturally drawn to kindness and can easily discern whether someone in our network is selfless or selfish. Simple acts of kindness strengthen the bonds of trust and mutual respect in a relationship.

Creating time to be with friends and family is vital to nurturing relationships. While gifts and money have their place, they can never replace the value of your presence and the memories you create with those in your network. It's essential to be intentional about planning time to spend with your loved ones. As you schedule your work tasks and daily activities, you should also allocate time to cherish and nurture your relationships. Building strong connections requires time, and making it a priority will strengthen the bonds.

Maintaining friendships and relationships is not effortless—it requires work and dedication. Unfortunately, some people only reach out to their friends or family when they need something, which can come across as being selfish. This approach often leads to strained relationships and a lack of genuine connection. Instead, consider regularly reaching out to check on those in your network, simply to ask how they are doing. Doing so demonstrates that you value them as individuals, not just as resources or as an **"Automated Teller Machine (ATM)"**. This effort to connect with them without an ulterior motive fosters trust and goodwill, making it easier to receive support when you genuinely need it.

BE HONEST AND TRUSTWORTHY

Honesty is the quality of being truthful, sincere, and free from deceit. It means consistently telling the truth and acting in a way that reflects transparency and integrity. Being honest builds trust with others because they can rely on your words and actions to be genuine. You are honest and trustworthy when your words and your actions align.

In any relationship, whether personal or professional, honesty and trustworthiness are cornerstones that strengthen the connection. When people know they can trust you, they are more likely to support, invest, and collaborate with you. In the journey toward wealth and success, honesty and reliability in your dealings can open doors that might otherwise remain closed. Trust cannot be bought or easily repaired once broken;

it must be consistently earned and maintained through your actions.

Honesty is a valuable asset. It will make others eager to lend you their support when you need it, just as the widow in our earlier story found help from her neighbours. In the world of business and personal growth, a reputation for honesty can set you apart, making people want to engage with you and assist in your endeavours. Cherish this quality, for it is a foundation upon which solid and lasting relationships are built.

Honesty, trust, and integrity are tightly interwoven and may be difficult to separate. These qualities are not just moral ideals; they are practical tools that shape our relationships, reputation, and even our success. In my culture, there's a wise saying: *"Do not soil your father's name."* This saying highlights the importance of maintaining integrity, urging us to protect our family's reputation and never to exchange it for material gain. It serves as a reminder that integrity is far more valuable than any material gain. While money can be lost and regained, a tarnished reputation may take a lifetime to rebuild, if it can be rebuilt at all. Therefore, it's crucial to prioritise your integrity above all else, refusing to compromise it for any temporary benefit.

Integrity is not just about how we interact with others; it starts with how we treat ourselves. When we think of integrity, we often consider it in the context of our relationships with others—being truthful, reliable, and consistent. However, integrity begins with you. It involves being true to yourself and your commitments and values. If you promise yourself that you'll wake up at 5 a.m. or commit to reading a book, for instance, maintaining integrity means following through, even when it's difficult. This is foundational because it sets the standard for approaching other areas of life. When you are honest with yourself and honour your commitments, extending that same integrity to others becomes second nature.

Developing personal integrity could be likened to forming a habit. Habits take time to establish, but once ingrained, they guide your actions almost automatically. You form a habit, but it takes the wheel and moulds you later. If you consistently practice integrity in minor things—like keeping promises to yourself—it becomes easier to maintain integrity in major, more challenging situations. Over time, this habit of integrity shapes who you are, making you a person others can trust and rely on.

THE POWER OF RELATIONSHIPS AND INTEGRITY: A REAL-LIFE SUCCESS STORY

I recently heard the story of a business tycoon, which I found very inspiring. This story also illustrates how relationships and integrity can turn seemingly impossible situations into incredible success stories. The story revolves around the challenges and triumphs of Engineer Charles Aladewolu, a Nigerian entrepreneur, and demonstrates the true value of trust, persistence, and the power of a good network.

I was so inspired and amazed by his story that I watched the video and listened to his words several times. The more I listened, the more I saw the wisdom of a man who has left a lasting mark on history. A part of his story resonates with what we are discussing in this chapter, and I would like you to learn from it. I have tried to present the story in his words. You will definitely find it valuable.

"I'm unsure how many of you are familiar with mobile masts. If you go near a stadium, you'll notice large, expensive masts with antennas and other equipment mounted. These masts are crucial because when many people gather in one place, like a stadium, you often experience dropped calls and network inefficiencies. The masts help manage the load by boosting the signal in those areas.

Now, consider how many football matches are played monthly in a stadium in Nigeria. Sometimes, there might not be a single match the entire month. A European company saw this and thought, "Why not make these masts mobile?" With mobile masts, you can move them from one stadium to another as needed. For example, if there's a match in Lagos Stadium today and another one in two days at a different location, you can simply drive the mast to the next venue. It's a brilliant idea. I promoted this concept in Nigeria, and a company decided to purchase 12 units from us. It was an exciting opportunity, but there was a catch—they wouldn't pay a dime until all 12 units were delivered to their warehouse.

I discussed this with my partners in Europe, and they insisted on an irrevocable letter of credit before they could manufacture or ship the units. So, I went to the bank to request the letter of credit. The manager checked our company account and, upon seeing the balance, laughed. It was clear that we didn't have enough funds to secure the letter of credit. I explained that we needed a loan to complete the contract, but even then, the interest rate was 28%, and they required a certificate of occupancy for properties in high-value areas like Victoria Island, which I didn't have. In the end, the deal failed.

But I wasn't ready to give up. I remembered that the Holy Spirit is my senior business partner, and I believe nothing is impossible with Him. So, I went into prayer, and the Holy Spirit guided me to approach my European partners and ask them to manufacture and ship the equipment without a letter of credit. The idea seemed impossible, but I trusted that it could be done if the Holy Spirit said it could be done.

I flew to Holland, and when I met with my partners, they were excited, thinking I had brought the letter of credit. But they were stunned when I told them of my proposal—to manufacture and ship everything to Nigeria without an LC, with payment to be made only after delivery. Initially, they rejected the idea, saying it was too risky. They couldn't even imagine doing such a thing for a European company, let alone one in Africa.

Feeling overwhelmed, I excused myself to the restroom and prayed again. The Holy Spirit reassured me, telling me to sit back and allow Him to work. When I returned to the meeting, the atmosphere had shifted. The owner of the company spoke up, saying, "Charles is not just a customer; he's a partner we trust." He accepted the proposal, and the deal was sealed just like that.

The equipment was manufactured and shipped to Nigeria. When it arrived, I faced another challenge—I didn't have the money to clear the shipment. My wife suggested using the same faith-based approach with the clearing agent. I proposed paying him a 10% commitment fee, and he agreed to clear the equipment and deliver it to the customer's warehouse. Everything worked out smoothly.

The customer's engineer inspected the equipment and issued a certificate of acceptance, after which the payment was made exactly 15 days later, as per the contract. I then returned to the bank that had refused to help me earlier, with three envelopes in hand. Upon seeing the substantial amount in our account, the manager was shocked. He locked his office door and asked me to pray for him.

I used the first envelope to pay the suppliers, the second to pay the clearing agent, and the third to pay my employees."[15]

This story demonstrates the value of networks, relationships, trust, honesty, and integrity. Without any of these, he would not have been able to complete the project. By cherishing and nurturing your relationships while maintaining honesty and integrity, you build a foundation that can withstand even the most challenging circumstances.

As we conclude this chapter, it's clear that the connections you build and the integrity you maintain are crucial to your success. Your relationships and integrity can open doors that money alone cannot.

But our journey doesn't end here. In the next chapter, "Understanding Bad and Good Debts," we will delve into the crucial difference between debts that propel you forward and those that can hold you back. Get ready to uncover how leveraging the right kind of debt can be a powerful tool in building wealth while learning to avoid the pitfalls of bad debt that can derail your progress. Continue reading, as you don't want to miss the information in the new chapter.

KEY EIGHT

Understanding Bad And Good Debts

We have come a long way in this wealth creation journey, and I commend you for your commitment to success. You are truly remarkable for reading and taking steps toward your financial success. This new chapter will explore the 8th key to moving from debt to wealth—or increasing your wealth if you're already on that path. This key is all about understanding the difference between bad and good debts. If there are bad debts, there must surely be good ones. We'll dive into the difference shortly.

In the story we have been considering, the prophet instructed the poor widow, "Borrow as many empty jars as you can from your friends and neighbours."[1] Now, think about this—she was already in debt, yet the prophet told her to borrow more. Wasn't that piling debt upon debt? She was in a financial mess, yet this advice led to her ultimate liberation. This example clearly shows that all debts are not the same. There are bad debts, which can drag one down, and good debts, which can be instrumental in building wealth. So, what exactly are these good and bad debts? Let's check them out.

First, I am not a certified financial expert, and the insights shared in this chapter regarding debt are based on my personal views and experiences. While I hope these perspectives offer valuable guidance, I strongly recommend that you consult with a qualified financial advisor before making any decisions about debt and its management.

Debts can impact your financial journey either positively or otherwise. Therefore, understanding the dynamics of debt is essential to your financial success.

Now, let us consider bad debts. Bad debts drain your resources without providing any potential for future income or growth. In simple terms, bad debt takes money away from you. It does not bring money; instead, it drains you of your money. These are typically debts incurred to purchase items that depreciate in value, such as shoes, wears and other consumer goods, luxury items, or even vacations. While these may bring temporary pleasure, they do not contribute to your financial well-being in the long term. Also, bad debts often come with high interest rates and can quickly spiral out of control, leading to a cycle of debt that is hard to escape. The simple test is this: Before taking a loan, ask yourself, 'Will this loan bring money into my pocket or take money away from me?' Your answer will inform you whether it's a good or bad debt.

On the other hand, good debts have the potential to generate income or appreciate in value over time. It has the potential to increase your income. It could be borrowing to start a business like the woman in the above story. She borrowed jars for her business. What she borrowed could be referred to as her seed capital - the capital needed to start a business. It could also be a loan to get a property that appreciates in time or a mortgage for a home. Good debts can be seen as tools that, when managed wisely, can help you build wealth. They allow you to leverage other people's money to create value, grow your assets, and ultimately achieve financial freedom. The key is to use good debts strategically, ensuring that the return on investment outweighs the cost of borrowing.

Wait a minute, can a seemingly good debt turn bad? Absolutely! A debt that starts out as good can turn bad if not appropriately managed. This is why financial literacy is crucial—you must be able to calculate the numbers, understand the risks involved, and evaluate the potential returns. One of the important questions to ask yourself before taking on any debt is: "Will the returns from this loan cover the loan payments over its lifetime and also yield benefits?" If the answer is uncertain or negative, what seems like a good debt could quickly become a financial burden.

Take, for example, a business loan. Borrowing money to expand your business might seem like a good debt because it can increase your income. However, if the business fails to generate the expected profits or if market conditions change unfavourably, that same loan can become a heavy financial burden. The income generated by the business may no longer be sufficient to cover the loan repayments, turning what was once a good debt into a bad one.

Similarly, consider a mortgage on a property. Buying a home is typically considered a good debt because real estate generally appreciates over time. However, the debt can become unmanageable if the property market crashes or the borrower loses their job and can no longer make mortgage payments. The borrower may find themselves in a situation where they owe more on the mortgage than the property is worth, known as being "underwater" on the loan. In such cases, a good debt can quickly become a financial nightmare.

Another crucial factor to consider when evaluating debt is the interest rate attached to the loan. In our earlier story, the widow borrowed empty jars from her neighbours at a zero per cent interest rate, meaning she didn't have to repay more than she borrowed. This lack of interest allowed her to maximise profits and successfully overcome financial hardship. In contrast, taking on a loan with a high interest rate can significantly increase the cost of borrowing and reduce the potential returns on your investment. Even if you intend to use the loan for a promising business venture, exorbitant interest rates can erode your profits and turn what seemed like a good debt into a detrimental one.

For instance, imagine an entrepreneur who takes out a substantial loan to start a new business, believing that the venture will generate enough income to cover the loan repayments and yield profit. However, if the loan has a high interest rate, a significant portion of the business earnings will go toward paying interest alone. This financial strain can dwarf the growth of the business, making it difficult to reinvest profits or cover operational costs. Sometimes, the business may not generate enough revenue to keep up with the mounting interest payments, leading to default and potential bankruptcy. This example illustrates how imperative it is to thoroughly assess and negotiate interest rates before committing to any form of debt, ensuring that the cost of borrowing does not outweigh the anticipated benefits.

Assets And Liabilities

It is also suitable for you to understand these terms: Assets and Liabilities. An asset is anything that puts money into your pocket, such as owning a rental property that generates income, stocks that pay dividends, or a business that earns profits. On the other hand, a liability is anything that takes money out of your pocket, like a car loan, credit card debt, or a mortgage on a home that doesn't generate income. Understanding the difference between these two is essential because it shapes how you manage your finances and ultimately determines whether you move closer to wealth or fall deeper into debt.

To stay above financial stress, the value of your assets must outweigh your liabilities. In other words, what you own should generate more income than what you owe or spend. If your liabilities exceed your assets, it's time to reassess and find ways to either reduce your liabilities or convert them into assets. For instance, consider your car—does it bring in money, or is it just another expense? If it only costs you maintenance, insurance, and fuel, then it's a liability. However, if you use your car for a rideshare service or to deliver goods, it can become an asset that generates income. The key is to live within your current financial means while consistently working to build and increase your assets. This approach will gradually lead you to the financial freedom you desire.

FINANCIAL FREEDOM

Before diving deeper into the concept of financial freedom, it's essential to understand the two types of income: active and passive. Active income is the revenue you earn directly from your work. This means that without your ongoing effort, the income stops. For example, your salary is a form of active income—you work for a certain number of hours, and in return, you receive a paycheck. On the other hand, passive income is the revenue that continues to flow in without your direct involvement after you've set up the necessary systems. Examples include royalties from a product, such as a book or an online course, or income generated from a rental property.

The key to financial freedom is building enough passive income to exceed expenses. Imagine your monthly expenses amount to $2,000, and you have assets generating $2,500 in passive income every month. With this setup, you no longer need to work out of necessity, as your passive income covers all your expenses, allowing you to work by choice rather than obligation. This shift from reliance on active income to passive income is the foundation of financial freedom—it's about creating a financial system that sustains your lifestyle without the constant need for your labour.

Unfortunately, many people find themselves stuck in jobs they dislike, not because they want to be there but because they have bills to pay, and without the job, the bills cannot be paid. This forces them to stay in positions that offer little or no fulfilment or happiness. I've experienced this myself, even as a medical doctor. I was once on a job that took away over 80 hours of my time per week, leaving me with no time for anything else. I was inspired to write a book from this past experience titled "**FIND YOUR WORK: Unlocking Your Path to Impact, Fulfilment, and Worthy Compensation.**" In it, I share my journey and offer insights on how to discover work that pays the bills, brings fulfilment, and allows you to make a meaningful impact. If this resonates with you, I encourage you to get a copy (https://pnuxelconsulting.com/fyw) or visit your favourite bookstore.

It would help if you strived to attain financial freedom where your passive income comfortably covers your expenses, granting you the freedom to live life on your terms to impact your world and not out of pressure and obligation to pay bills.

Using Other People's Money (OPM) for Wealth Creation

The concept of "Other People's Money" (OPM) is a wealth creation strategy that allows you to leverage resources beyond your own to build and grow financial assets. Simply put, OPM refers to using borrowed funds or investments from others to finance your ventures rather than relying solely on your personal savings or income. This approach enables you to undertake larger projects or investments than you could afford on your own, potentially amplifying your returns and accelerating your path to wealth.

For example, consider a real estate investor who wants to purchase a rental property. Instead of using their own money to buy the property outright, they might crowdfund the project, promising a return to those involved. By doing this, they use the people's money to acquire the property while only contributing a fraction of the cost as a down payment. The rental income generated from tenants can then be used to pay off borrowed money and compensate those involved, with any additional profit contributing to their financial success. This way, the investor leverages OPM to increase their assets and build wealth.

While leveraging Other People's Money (OPM) can significantly boost your wealth-building efforts, it's crucial to understand the risks involved and take necessary precautions. Like any financial strategy, OPM requires careful planning and thorough research. If not managed wisely, borrowing funds or relying on external investments can lead to financial strain, potentially jeopardizing your integrity and placing undue pressure on your finances. Before diving into any OPM strategy, ensure you have a solid plan in place and fully understand the potential risks and rewards.

A company selling shares to the public is similar to the OPM strategy in action. When a company issues shares, it's essentially raising capital from investors to fund its operations, expand its business, or develop new products. In return, the investors receive dividends and partial ownership of the company. This allows the company to access substantial funds without taking on debt, while investors benefit from the company's growth and profitability.

Another practical example of OPM is requesting a down payment for a project or service. Suppose you've been contracted to complete a large project. Instead of financing the entire project out of your pocket, you could ask for a down payment from the client. This upfront payment provides the capital needed to start the project, reducing your financial pressure. Once the project is completed, you receive the remaining payment, which includes your profit. This approach minimises your financial exposure while ensuring you have the resources to deliver quality work.

As we wrap up this chapter on understanding bad and good debts, remember that the insights you've gained here are not just theoretical—they are practical tools you can apply immediately to improve your finances. Remember, the road to financial freedom is a journey, and each key we've explored brings you one step closer to the goal.

Once again, we are not at the end of our exploration yet. The next chapter will dive into Key 9: Avoid Distractions. In today's fast-paced world, staying focused on your goals is more challenging than ever. Distractions come in many forms, and if not managed properly, they can derail even the most well-laid plans. In the upcoming chapter, you'll learn how to avoid distractions. Get ready to discover the secrets to maintaining laser-like focus and pushing through to the finish line. You won't want to miss this! Let us get started.

KEY NINE

Avoid Distractions

Ideas often emerge when your mind is quiet and free from distractions. Imagine ten people talking to you simultaneously, all wanting to be heard. How would you feel? How much could you truly grasp from each person? That happens when you're distracted; your ability to focus and extract value diminishes. It is, therefore, crucial for you to learn how to avoid distractions.

It was not out of place when the prophet told the poor widow to close the door behind herself before pouring the oil from the flask into the jars. This act was symbolic—a clear message that avoiding distractions is crucial to getting the 'oil of ideas' flowing.

We have seen previously that ideas are crucial to success, and your journey to outstanding financial success and fulfilment comes with converting your ideas into valuable assets. Imagine being too distracted to get the ideas in the first place. What if the difference between your current situation and your breakthrough lies in your ability to avoid distractions and take bold, calculated risks?

Identifying And Eliminating Distractions

The present century may be referred to as the most distracted, and it's easy to see why. With the proliferation of smartphones, social media, and other digital technologies, it's easier than ever to get sidetracked and lose focus. It's not uncommon for you to feel overwhelmed by the constant stream of notifications, messages, and emails coming at you from all sides.

One of the key steps in staying focused and avoiding distractions is identifying what is causing those distractions in the first place. This can be challenging, as distractions come in many forms and may be subtle. However, with some awareness and some self-reflection, you can start to identify the sources of your distractions and take steps to eliminate them.

In my tribe, it is said that "A problem is half-solved when it is identified." That's why it's so important to recognise the things that distract you—once we do, we're already halfway to solving the problem.

For example, if you find that you're constantly distracted by your phone's notifications, you might consider turning off those notifications or setting specific times of the day to check your phone. Suppose you're struggling to focus because of the constant emails in your inbox. You might consider setting up automated responses or using your email application's "do not disturb" feature.

Here are some tips for identifying distractions.

1. **Start by listing all the things that distract you.** This might include phone notifications, emails, social media, chatty coworkers or friends, or anything else that takes your focus away from your work.

2. **Next, consider how often these distractions occur.** Are they constant interruptions, or do they only happen occasionally? Are they more likely to happen at certain times of the day? Understanding the frequency and timing of your distractions can help you identify patterns and plan accordingly.

3. **Once you have a list of your distractions, it's time to start brainstorming ways to eliminate them.** For example, if you're constantly distracted by phone notifications, you might consider turning off those notifications or

setting specific times of the day to check the phone.

4. **Don't be afraid to experiment with different strategies for eliminating distractions.** What works for one person might not work for you, so be willing to try different approaches and see what works best for you. With a little effort, you'll be able to identify the distractions holding you back and take steps to eliminate them.

Now that you have identified the distractions that interfere with your productivity. It is time to eliminate them. Here are some tips for doing that, thus boosting your productivity and putting yourself on the path to success.

1. Start by listing the distractions you've identified above and the strategies you've devised to eliminate them. This will help you keep track of

your progress and stay motivated as you work to eliminate them.

2. Begin implementing your strategies one at a time, starting with the distractions that have the biggest impact on your productivity. For example, if you find that notifications on your phone are a constant distraction, you might start by turning off those notifications, putting on the focus mode on your phone, or setting specific times of the day to check your phone.

3. As you work to eliminate your distractions, be mindful of your habits and behaviours. Are there times of the day when you're more prone to getting sidetracked? Are there certain tasks that are particularly difficult for you to focus on? By understanding your tendencies, you can tailor your strategies to suit your needs better.

4. Don't be afraid to seek help if you're struggling to eliminate a particular distraction. This might

involve seeking advice from a mentor or coach, asking a coworker for support, or even seeking the guidance of a professional therapist.

5. Finally, remember to be patient with yourself. Eliminating distractions isn't a one-time task but a continuous process of self-improvement. With time and practice, you'll better identify and eliminate distractions and focus on what matters most.

Useful Tools To Help You Eliminate Distractions.

Many tools are available to help you avoid digital distractions and stay focused on your work. Some options include

1. **Website blockers:** Tools like Freedom (https://freedom.to/) and Cold Turkey (https://getcoldturkey.com) allow you to block access to distracting websites or apps during specific times of the day. For example, use a

Avoid Distractions

website blocker to block social media during work hours or prevent yourself from getting distracted by online shopping while trying to focus on a project.

2. **Time tracking apps:** Tools like Toggl (https://toggl.com) and RescueTime (https://www.rescuetime.com/) allow you to track how much time you're spending on different tasks and websites, giving you a better understanding of where your time is going as time is a resource that should be invested and not wasted. You can use this information to identify your most common distractions and take steps to eliminate them. What you put your time into or how you invest your time determines your success: this is the differentiating factor between successful individuals and those that are not.

3. **"Do not disturb" features:** Many apps and devices, including smartphones and computers,

have a "do not disturb" feature that allows you to silence notifications or block incoming calls and messages during specific times of the day. This can be especially helpful if you're working on a task that requires intense focus.

4. **Noise-cancelling headphones:** If you're easily distracted by noise or chatter, noise-cancelling headphones can be a lifesaver. These headphones use advanced technology to block out external noise, allowing you to focus on your work without being interrupted by your surroundings. You can check the appropriate store to get one.

5. **Focus music:** Apps like Focus@Will (https://www.focusatwill.com/) and Noisli (https://www.noisli.com/) offer a selection of background music and sounds designed to help you focus and block out distractions.

Please familiarise yourself with the tools and use them as and when due.

APART FROM THE ABOVE, HERE IS THE GREATEST TOOL I HAVE FOUND IN ELIMINATING DISTRACTIONS.

In the previous sections, we've covered a range of strategies for staying focused and avoiding distractions. All of these strategies are important for staying on track and making progress towards your goals, but there's one tool that I've found particularly effective in eliminating distractions. You may be wondering what this tool is and how to engage it. I will share this all-time effective tool in this section and how to effectively engage it. Before I mention the tool, let's lay the foundation to understand the tool better. So, let's get started!

As you may know, discipline is the practice of training your mind and actions to follow a set of rules or a specific course of action. It involves developing good habits, setting boundaries, and adhering to standards or expectations. This is especially important to stay on track and achieve a set goal. *The antidote to distraction is discipline: being able to do what you are supposed to do at the right time and place.* If you are not unnecessarily distracted, then you are disciplined. It takes discipline to stay on track, as there will always be things that will compete for your attention.

There is more to discipline than the above, as the force behind it can be within or without. This leads us to the subject called **self-discipline.** When the force behind keeping you on track to success is within, it is called self-discipline. Self-discipline is the ability to control your thoughts, actions, and behaviours all by yourself. It involves setting goals and working towards them without being pushed by anyone, even when you don't feel like it or when there are distractions around you. Self-discipline is often considered a key component of success and can be especially important for you if you want to stay focused and on track.

One striking difference between discipline and self-discipline is that discipline is often imposed from the outside, while self-discipline is self-motivated. For example, discipline might be imposed by a teacher, parent, or boss, while self-discipline comes from within.

Additionally, discipline tends to focus on following rules or standards, while self-discipline focuses more on personal growth and achievement.

Another difference between discipline and self-discipline is that discipline tends to be more reactive, while self-discipline is proactive. Discipline is often used to correct or prevent negative behaviours, while self-discipline is proactively working towards a specific goal or objective and avoiding negative behaviours that will deter the individual from achieving the goals.

Again, discipline and self-discipline can have different effects on your overall well-being. Discipline may be seen as a form of punishment or control, which can lead to feelings of resentment or frustration. Self-discipline, on the other hand, can lead to a sense of accomplishment and personal growth, helping you feel more fulfilled and satisfied with your life and work.

Thus far, we have considered various tools like web blockers, time-tracking apps and devices with "do not disturb" features that can help eliminate distractions. However, I have found one tool which stands above the rest when it comes to eliminating distractions and is thus the greatest of all. It is nothing but *self-discipline fueled by a passion for a lifetime vision or goal.*

Self-discipline is the most powerful discipline on earth, and there is no greater self-discipline than one driven by a passion or inner strength to achieve a lifetime goal or vision. When you are convinced and passionate about a lifetime vision, you will be self-disciplined and able to overcome any form of distraction. This is the most incredible tool of all. Prayer and fasting can't do what this tool can. The answer to your prayers and fasting for overcoming distractions is insight and passion for a lifetime goal and vision. Without self-discipline fueled by a passion for a goal, every other tool to eliminate distractions will fail as it is a matter of time.

No motivational force can be compared to the energy or passion for achieving a lifetime goal or vision. Nothing can quench such motivation as long as the individual is convinced of it.

Conviction about a lifetime or short-term goal is more than just talking about it. It is an inner energy and belief in the vision. Anyone who gets to this point can discipline themselves to align appropriately to achieve the vision.

Passion is a strong and intense emotion or enthusiasm for something. It's a feeling that drives you to pursue your interests with energy and dedication. Passion is a powerful source of motivation, helping you stay focused and committed to your goals. The energy derived from passion can break boundaries and go through any problematic situation. A passionate man cannot be discouraged because their source of courage is within and not from their outer environment. The only thing that can stop a passionate man is discouragement from within. As long as they do not lose sight of what they have seen about themselves that others have not seen, they cannot be discouraged. Interestingly, what is supposed to be a discouragement to them fuels them to action and gives them more energy as they see it as a motivation to their goals.

History is full of passionate men who tread the paths of difficulty and discouragement in strength and courage because they were convinced of their life vision and goals. *One thing is common to them; they are self-disciplined*. They need no one to tell them what they are supposed to do because their motivation is from within. While no one watches, they get to work and are not easily distracted.

Passion can fuel self-discipline by providing a strong sense of purpose or meaning. When you're passionate about something, you're more likely to be motivated to work towards the goal, even when it's not easy. Additionally, passion can help you stay focused and avoid getting sidetracked by distractions, as you're more likely to be engaged and invested in your work. Passionate individuals do not have the time for gossip, unnecessary chats and other distractions since their goals are usually bigger than them, and they are pressed to make every minute count to achieve the goals. They work as though the time allocated to them is not enough to achieve their goals; thus, they are buried in their work and are not easily sidetracked. So if you are distracted and have tried several strategies with no success, here is the ultimate solution: self-discipline fuelled by a passion for a lifetime vision. Every other thing falls in place when you get this right.

Here are a few ways in which passion can help you eliminate distractions:

1. **Passion provides motivation:** When you're passionate about your goals, you're more likely to work towards them, even when you're busy or overwhelmed. This can help you stay focused and avoid getting sidetracked by distractions.

2. **Passion helps you stay engaged:** When you're passionate about your goals, you're more likely to be engaged and invested in your work. It is said that 'Empty Barrels Make the Most Noise.' Passion for a lifetime goal keeps you engaged and unavailable for distractions.

3. **Passion helps you stay committed:** Passion can help you stay committed to your goals despite setbacks or obstacles. By staying committed and focused on your passion, you can eliminate distractions and progress toward your goals. Your lifetime goals allow you to direct your efforts and short-term goals toward an ultimate one.

4. **Passion provides a sense of purpose:** When you're passionate about your goals, it gives a sense of purpose and meaning. This can help you stay focused and motivated, even when facing challenges or distractions. This explains why some people render service without seeking payment, for instance. They are not motivated by the money rendered but by the joy and fulfilment they derive in their service: they have found meaning in their actions. No motivation can be compared to this.

5. **Passion helps you stay organised:** You're more likely to be organised and prepared when you're passionate about your goals and vision. This can help you stay on top of your tasks and avoid distractions. The thoughts of your goals take you over, make you work, and get you prepared and organised.

Self-discipline fuelled by a passion for a lifetime vision is a powerful tool for eliminating distractions and staying focused on your work and goals. By finding something you're passionate about and working towards it with dedication and self-discipline, you can stay motivated and on track, no matter what challenges or distractions come your way.

For more insights on avoiding distractions, check out my book, **"FROM OVERWHELMED TO ORGANIZED: A Time Management Blueprint for Busy Professionals."** You can purchase a copy through this link https://www.amazon.co.uk/dp/B0BSVHBLFV or from your favourite bookstore. It's also available in audio format—simply visit your preferred audiobook store, as it's distributed globally.

GUARD YOUR MORNINGS

We have established that successfully managing distractions is crucial for success. Many successful individuals guard their mornings with great care, understanding that these moments set the tone for everything that follows. When you wake up, your mind is at its freshest, making it the ideal time to focus on your ideas and plan your day. Instead of diving into the chaos of notifications and messages, consider using this quiet time to outline your goals, prioritise tasks, and set a clear direction for your day.

Starting your morning with a well-thought-out plan can be the difference between a productive day and one lost to distractions. The saying, "If you fail to plan, you plan to fail," holds true.

GET AWAY FROM THE CROWD

The prophet's instruction to the widow, "shut the door behind you"[1], demonstrates a profound lesson: sometimes, you need to step away from the crowd and noise to chart the way forward for your life. It might warrant physical separation from the crowd to create an enabling environment and mental space for creativity, strategic thinking and innovation. In a world full of distractions, carving out quiet time can be the difference between staying stuck and breaking through to new levels of success.

Stepping away from the crowd allows you to recharge and strategies. Regularly scheduling time to be alone with your thoughts is important for wealth creation. This time alone is for deep reflection, planning, and innovation. When you emerge from these moments of solitude, you will often find that your ideas are sharper, your goals clearer, and your motivation renewed. People will notice the difference in you, even if they can't quite put their finger on what has changed.

Retreats, whether a few hours or days, are invaluable for this kind of personal growth. By withdrawing from the usual environment, you give yourself the space to think differently, see new perspectives, and make better decisions. These retreats can be as simple as a weekend in a quiet place or as structured as a formal personal retreat. The key is to disconnect from the usual distractions and reconnect with your purpose.

Additionally, learn to work in silence. The best ideas often come when no one is watching, when you're grinding in the quiet moments, away from the crowd. The most successful people know the value of keeping their work under wraps until it's fully developed. By working in silence, you avoid premature criticism and protect your ideas until they're ready to be revealed.

If you're wondering how to effectively avoid distractions and maximise your productivity, you might find more insights in my book, "**From Overwhelmed to Organized: A Time Management Blueprint for Busy Professionals.**" It's full of practical tips and strategies for managing your time and energy so you can focus on what really matters.

Even Jesus, the great teacher, demonstrated the importance of retreat by dismissing the crowd and His disciples to be alone. This act was a deliberate choice to create space for reflection, prayer, and renewal. It underscores the power of stepping away from the crowd to connect with one's inner self and receive guidance.

Another powerful example is that of Elijah, who God summoned to the mountain. Despite the dramatic events—fire, earthquake, and wind—it was only in the gentle whisper that Elijah received the divine instructions he needed.

These stories illustrate a timeless truth: the most profound insights and instructions often come in moments of stillness, away from the noise and distractions of life. We cannot overemphasise the importance of avoiding distractions, getting away from the crowd, and engaging in personal retreats. These practices are essential ingredients for idea creation and, ultimately, wealth creation. So, make it a priority to get away from the crowd, create space for innovation, and listen for that gentle whisper that could guide you to your next big breakthrough.

As we wrap up this chapter on avoiding distractions, it's clear that the ability to focus, retreat, and tune out the noise is a necessity on your journey to financial freedom. Your ideas are precious, and protecting the space where they flourish is key to transforming them into valuable assets. *The quiet moments you carve out for yourself can be the difference between staying where you are and breaking through to new levels of success.*

The next chapter will delve into "Key 10: You Get Results to the Extent of Your Faith and Willingness to Take Calculated Risks." Are you ready to explore how your faith and risk-taking abilities can shape your financial destiny? Get ready because this next chapter will challenge you to step out of your comfort zone and take bold steps toward your dreams.

KEY TEN

You Get Results To The Extent Of Your Faith And Willingness To Take Calculated Risks

Do you know why the oil stopped flowing in the story of the prophet and the poor widow? Let us check. "Then go into your house with your sons and shut the door behind you. Pour olive oil from your flask into the jars, setting each one aside when it is filled." So she did as she was told. Her sons kept bringing jars to her, and she filled one after another. Soon every container was full to the brim! "Bring me another jar," she said to one of her sons. "There aren't any more!" he told her. And then the olive oil stopped flowing."[1]

This story teaches the relationship between faith, action, and results. The oil flowed as long as there were empty jars to fill, and it stopped only when no more vessels were left. This shows that the amount of oil the widow received was directly proportional to the number of empty jars she provided. If she had only brought one jar, that's all she would have gotten. But what if she had provided a field full of tanks or even a tank farm? The oil would have kept flowing until every single container was filled to the brim. This brings us to the tenth key in moving from debt to wealth and wealth creation: *You Get Results to the Extent of Your Faith and Willingness to Take Calculated Risks.*

Imagine yourself in the widow's situation. How many empty jars would you have gathered? Would you have been bold enough to believe that a small flask of oil could fill numerous large containers? It takes a certain level of faith to obey an instruction that seems illogical.

It's the same with your ideas. The potential of an idea, no matter how small it seems, is boundless. But the question is, do you have enough faith to believe in its growth? Do you have the courage to take calculated risks and make enough room for that idea to expand? Your results will always match the extent of your faith and the quantity of the **"empty jars"** you prepare.

In this context, faith isn't just about believing without seeing; it's about taking action based on your belief. Faith is not dormant but active. It's about preparing for abundance, even when scarcity is all you see. The widow could have hesitated, doubting whether it made sense to gather so many jars when she had only a small amount of oil. But she acted in faith, and her reward was a miracle of provision. Similarly, in your journey to wealth creation, you need to be ready to take bold steps—steps that may seem risky but are necessary if you're going to see extraordinary results.

The size of your success is often limited not by your circumstances but by your capacity to believe and take calculated risks. Are you willing to step out of your comfort zone, trust in the potential of your ideas, and prepare for the overflow? The more "empty jars" you gather—the more room you make for growth—the greater your rewards will be. So, how many jars are you ready to bring?

Don't Be Afraid To Fail.

Fear of failure is often one of the biggest obstacles that hold people back from achieving outstanding success. This fear can prevent you from taking the steps necessary to achieve your goals. However, as we've seen in the widow's story, the results come to those willing to take bold, calculated risks. Just as she had to gather as many jars as possible, despite the uncertainty of how much oil would flow, you too must be willing to step out in faith—even when failure seems like a possibility.

The truth is that failure is not an enemy. It's a necessary part of the journey to success. Every outstanding achievement has been accompanied by setbacks and lessons learned along the way. The key is not to let the fear of failure paralyse you. Instead, see failure as a stepping stone, a learning experience that brings you closer to your goal. Don't be afraid to fail!

Failure is ingrained in the fabric of success. It's almost impossible to find a great achievement that hasn't been preceded by some form of failure. It is true that our educational system often penalises failure, creating a mindset that failure is not allowed. This conditioning can be detrimental when it comes to real-world success, where taking risks and learning from failures are essential components of the journey. If you let the fear of failure instilled by the schooling system hold you back, you may never reach your full potential because you discover what truly works through experimentation and testing your ideas.

In the world of scientific research, there is room for failed experiments. Scientists understand that every experiment, even those that don't produce the desired results, brings them one step closer to a breakthrough. This approach should be applied to your journey in wealth creation and personal success. As Thomas Edison famously said, "I have not failed. I've just found 10,000 ways that won't work." Do not be afraid to test your ideas; you will recognise that each setback is a lesson moving you closer to your goal.

Embracing failure doesn't mean accepting mediocrity. You should always put your best effort into whatever you pursue. While doing so, maintain a positive mindset regardless of the outcome. If you encounter failure, remember that it doesn't define you. Instead, see it as a signal to return to the drawing board, make the necessary adjustments, and keep moving forward.

Don't let the fear of failure stop you from taking bold, calculated risks. The willingness to experiment, fail, and learn separates those who succeed from those who remain paralysed by fear. Every jar you gather in faith, even if it doesn't fill the way you expected, is part of the journey toward finding the one that will overflow with success.

We have seen that one of the essential keys to wealth creation is to embrace failure as a natural part of the journey toward success. The journey to success is not a straight line; it is curvy, with mountains, valleys, and pastures along the way.

Failures are not setbacks but stepping stones to growth and resilience. As the legendary basketball player Michael Jordan once said, *"I've missed more than 9,000 shots in my career. I've lost almost 300 games. Twenty-six times, I've been trusted to take the game-winning shot and missed. I've failed over and over and over again in my life. And that is why I succeed."*

Embracing failure means learning from mistakes, adapting, and persisting despite setbacks. It recognises that every stumble brings you closer to your goals, as Winston Churchill noted: *"Success is not final, failure is not fatal: It is the courage to continue that counts."*

When you view failure as a valuable teacher rather than an adversary, you nurture a positive mindset that thrives on resilience, perseverance, and the unwavering belief that setbacks are inscribed into the path to success.

It is good to know that failure is part of winning and not the opposite of winning.

THREE FEET AWAY FROM GOLD

A common reason for failure often lies in the inability to look beyond setbacks and discern opportunities when it is just around the corner. Albert Einstein put it this way, *"In the middle of every difficulty lies opportunity."*

The story of R. U. Darby, a highly successful insurance salesman, illustrates how he learned to bounce back from a devastating defeat and, more importantly, faith, courage and patience as he sought success and a good life.

During the gold rush era, Darby's uncle set off for the West with the grand ambition of striking it rich. Upon arriving in Colorado, he heard tales of daily gold discoveries and wasted no time staking his claim. Armed with a pick and shovel, he toiled tirelessly, driven by his boundless energy and enthusiasm.

Weeks of gruelling labour finally bore fruit as he uncovered glimmering specks in the mud. Elation washed over him as he realised his dream of wealth was within reach. But as he contemplated the potential of his discovery, he faced a harsh reality: extracting the ore required machinery and drilling equipment. Without hesitation, he buried the mine and returned to his home in Maryland.

First, he shared the exciting news with his nephew, Rill Darby, who, in turn, enlisted the help of friends and relatives to raise funds for the necessary equipment. With their equipment ready, Darby and his uncle returned to Colorado to resume mining. The initial ore they extracted confirmed that they had stumbled upon one of Colorado's richest veins. Encouraged by the returns, they continued to drill fervently. Then, unexplainably, the gold vein disappeared. They were left empty-handed despite their efforts to dig deeper and recover it.

Months of fruitless labour forced them to concede defeat and sell the mine and machinery. A junk dealer offered them a meagre sum, which they accepted gratefully. However, recognising the mine's potential, the dealer sought expert advice and discovered that the gold vein did not disappear but had merely shifted a few feet away. He resumed drilling and soon became a multi-millionaire.

Meanwhile, R. U. Darby had established a thriving insurance business. He harboured no self-pity or self-blame when he learned of the mine's newfound riches. Instead, he viewed his past failure as a valuable lesson. He had lost a vast fortune because he had stopped drilling just three feet from gold. Had he discerned that the opportunity was just 3 feet away? He resolved to apply this lesson to his sales career, vowing never to stop at "no." He would persistently try again and again.

This insight, gleaned from his failure, propelled Darby to become one of the most successful figures in the insurance industry. History teaches us that some of the most remarkable achievements arise from the ashes of profound defeats.

Do What You Haven't Done Before

If you want a different result, you might need to do things you've never done before. Albert Einstein famously said, *"Insanity is doing the same thing over and over again and expecting different results."* This truth resonates deeply in the journey of wealth creation and personal growth. If your current actions don't yield the desired results, it's time to step out of your comfort zone and try something new or take new actions.

Think about the story of the poor widow. She was instructed to gather as many jars as possible and pour oil into them. She had never done this, which required faith and willingness to take risks. But she achieved results she had never imagined—enough oil to sell and live on by doing what she had never done before. Her success was directly tied to her willingness to step into the unknown and trust the process.

To achieve the extraordinary, you must be willing to take unusual steps. This might mean acquiring new skills, exploring unfamiliar territories, or taking on challenges that initially seem daunting. It also means becoming someone new—a more resilient, more resourceful version of yourself who can handle the challenges that come with growth and success.

As you move forward, ask yourself: What have I not done before that could lead to my desired results? What changes do I need to make in myself to become the person who can achieve those results? Embrace the unfamiliar, take bold steps, and watch how your willingness to do what you haven't done before transforms your life.

As we close this chapter, remember that your results will always reflect the extent of your faith and your willingness to take calculated risks. Whether it's gathering more jars for the oil or daring to step into the unknown, your journey to wealth and fulfilment is about expanding your capacity and embracing the new. Don't shy away from failure—use it as a stepping stone, and be bold enough to do what you've never done before.

The next key is just as crucial. In the next chapter, we'll dive into the art of selling. Yes, to truly succeed, you must learn to be a salesperson—of your ideas, skills, and products, among others. Get ready to harness the power of salesmanship to propel yourself forward!

KEY ELEVEN

Be A Salesperson

I commend you for reading this far. This chapter centres on this book's next and 11th key to wealth creation. The key is as important as every other key because, without it, you would not earn money for your products and services—even if you have the finest product.

Did you know that the poor widow in the story we've been considering didn't initially know what to do with her jars filled with oil? She had followed the instructions, filled every jar, and created a valuable product. But after all that effort, she was at a loss for the next step. When she returned to Elisha for guidance, his advice was simple and powerful: "Now sell the olive oil and pay your debts, and you and your sons can live on what is left over."[1] This demonstrates the next key: be a salesperson. If you want to earn money, you must learn how to sell—you must be a salesperson.

Think about it: even if you have the most exceptional product in the world, if you don't know how to sell it, people are not likely to buy, and you won't receive the compensation you deserve for your labour. Selling isn't just about convincing people to buy something; it's about understanding your customers' needs, communicating the value of your product or service, and creating a connection that leads to a transaction.

To achieve financial success, you must embrace the role of a salesperson. This isn't just about having a product or service to offer; it's about mastering the art of selling itself. Whether you're selling your own goods, offering services, or promoting someone else's products, the key is to approach every transaction with a salesperson's mindset. No matter how innovative or valuable your product is, it won't generate income if it doesn't sell.

Selling is at the heart of wealth creation. Consider this: every successful entrepreneur or business mogul, at their core, is a salesperson. They understand that selling is more than just exchanging goods for money—it's about communicating value, building trust, and meeting the needs of others. When you sell, you're not just transferring a product; you're providing solutions, fulfilling desires, and creating connections that can lead to repeat business and referrals.

Moreover, being a salesperson doesn't always mean pushing a hard sell. It's about recognising opportunities where others see obstacles. It's about selling ideas to potential investors, selling your skills in a job interview, or even selling your vision to a team you're leading. The ability to sell is the bridge between having a great product or service and turning it into financial success.

Whether you're selling your own creations or someone else's, the principles remain the same. You must understand your market, know your product inside and out, and build relationships with your customers. Embrace the mindset that selling is an essential skill on your journey to wealth, and every sale brings you one step closer to your financial goals.

Don't Be Ashamed To Sell

Selling is an essential skill in the pursuit of wealth, yet many people feel hesitant or even ashamed to promote their products, services, or ideas. This hesitation often stems from a fear of rejection, judgment, or the misconception that selling is somehow beneath them. However, to achieve financial success, you must overcome these mental barriers. There's no shame in selling—instead, it's a powerful tool that can elevate your life and the lives of others.

Think about it: every successful entrepreneur began by selling something, from the corner store owner to the

CEO of a multinational corporation. Whether it's a tangible product, a service, or an idea, selling is the vehicle through which value is exchanged. Selling is not just about making money; it's about believing in what you have to offer and sharing that value with others. Embrace the process confidently, knowing that your selling ability is linked to wealth creation.

Don't be ashamed to sell. Selling isn't just about making money; it's about offering solutions to people who need them. Think about the everyday products you rely on—your phone, car, or favourite food. What if those items were created but never sold? You wouldn't have the convenience, comfort, or joy they bring to your life. Selling makes these products accessible to you, and it's the same for whatever you're offering.

Salespeople are not self-centred; they're problem-solvers. They identify needs and meet them with the right products or services. By selling, you're not imposing on others but serving them. You're providing something valuable that could improve their lives, solve problems, or fulfil needs. When you shift your mindset from "I need to sell" to "I'm offering something useful," selling becomes a service, not just a transaction.

Many hoard their gifts, products, and services out of fear or shame, but this mindset keeps them from reaching their full potential. It's time to break free from that mindset and recognise that your offering could be exactly what someone else is looking for. By marketing and selling your products, you're not only growing your wealth, but you're also helping others. When you sell, you do others a favour by making something valuable available to them.

Remember, the world is full of people looking for solutions, and you have the power to provide those solutions through your products and services. Don't let fear or shame stop you from putting yourself out there. Embrace the role of a salesperson with pride, knowing that you're positively impacting others' lives.

A Simple Guide To Overcoming The Fear Of Selling

Here's a five-point simple guide to overcoming shame in selling:

1. **Believe in the Value of What You Are Offering:** The first step to overcoming shame in selling is to have an unwavering belief in the value of what you're offering. When you know that your product, service, or idea can genuinely help others, it becomes easier to share it confidently. Understand that you're providing a solution, not just making a transaction.

2. **Shift from selling to serving:** Shift your mindset from "selling" to "serving." When you view selling as a way to serve others by meeting their needs or solving their problems, it removes the stigma and adds purpose to your efforts. You're not just pushing a product but making a positive impact.

3. **Practice and Prepare:** Like any other skill, selling becomes easier with practice. Role-play sales scenarios, rehearse your pitch, and prepare for common objections. The more comfortable and prepared you are, the less room there is for doubt and shame.

4. **Focus on the Customer's Needs:** Make the conversation about your customer, not about you. When you focus on understanding and meeting their needs, the pressure on you diminishes. This shift in focus allows you to connect more deeply and genuinely, making the sales process feel more natural and less intimidating.

5. **Learn from Rejection:** Rejection is a natural part of selling, but it doesn't define your worth or the value of what you're offering. Instead of feeling ashamed, use rejection as a learning opportunity. Each "no" can bring you closer to a "yes" if you take the time to analyse feedback,

adjust your approach, and keep moving forward.

5 ESSENTIAL ATTRIBUTES OF A SUCCESSFUL SALESPERSON

Here are five essential attributes of a successful salesperson. While more attributes could be considered, mastering these five will give you an advantage as a salesperson.

1. **Confidence:** Confidence is key in sales. When you believe in your product or service, it shows. Confidence reassures potential customers that they're making a good decision. Practice your pitch, know your product inside and out, and walk into every conversation with the mindset that your offering is valuable.

2. **Empathy:** Successful salespeople understand their customers' needs and concerns. They listen carefully and put themselves in the customer's shoes. Empathy allows you to tailor your

approach, address specific pain points, and build genuine relationships with clients.

3. **Resilience:** Sales can be tough, with plenty of rejections along the way. A successful salesperson doesn't let a "no" discourage them. Instead, they view rejection as an opportunity to learn, refine their approach, and move on to the next prospect with renewed determination.

4. **Adaptability:** The ability to adapt to different situations and personalities is crucial in sales. No two customers are the same, so being flexible in your approach will help you connect with a wider audience. This might mean adjusting your pitch, finding new ways to communicate value, or being open to feedback.

5. **Persistence:** Persistence is about following up and staying engaged without being pushy. It's knowing when to check in with a potential customer and not giving up too easily. Many

sales are made after several points of contact, so persistence can be the difference between closing a deal and losing it.

To truly excel as a salesperson, continuous learning is essential. Invest time in reading books and taking courses in sales. The more knowledge you acquire, the more effective you'll become at sales. Don't hesitate to leverage the expertise of others—seek mentorship from successful salespeople or join communities where you can exchange ideas and strategies.

Remember, the sales world is dynamic, and staying stagnant can cost you opportunities. Embrace change and be open to refining your techniques, adapting to new trends, and improving yourself and your products.

As we conclude this chapter, remember that being a salesperson is not just about making money; it's about providing value, solving problems, and serving others. Embrace the art of selling confidently, knowing that your products, services, and ideas can genuinely improve the lives of those you reach. You've come this far on your journey to wealth, and each key you've mastered brings you closer to achieving your goals.

Now, get ready to dive into the next and final chapter, where we'll explore "Key 12: Manage Your Resources." This chapter will show you how to make the most of what you have, ensuring that your hard-earned wealth is preserved and multiplied. You don't want to miss it!

KEY TWELVE

Manage Your Resources

Congratulations on making it this far in the journey toward your financial empowerment and personal growth. Your commitment to reading this far demonstrates your desire for self-improvement. This chapter, "Key 12: Manage Your Resources," is essential as it centres on a critical aspect of wealth preservation and multiplication.

Just as the prophet instructed the widow to sell the olive oil and live on what was left, the key lesson here is the importance of managing your resources. Much like your resources, the oil will eventually run out if you do not find ways to increase and sustain it. The widow and her sons might have been relieved of their immediate debt, but they risked falling back into debt without a strategy to multiply what was left.

In the same way, if you don't learn to reinvest, grow, and effectively manage your resources, you might find yourself back at square one despite temporary success. It would help if you cultivated the habit of multiplying what you have.

Resource management is not just about making money; it's about what you do with it once you have it. When you experience profit, spending it all is tempting, especially if you've worked hard for it. However, viewing your profits as seeds rather than spoils is crucial. Seeds are meant to be planted and nurtured so they can multiply. If you consume all your seeds, you won't have anything left to plant for future growth. Similarly, if you spend all your profits without reinvesting a portion, you're missing out on the opportunity to multiply your wealth.

Reinvesting your profits is a key principle of wealth creation. This doesn't necessarily mean returning all your money to the same venture. You might consider another venture. Whether expanding your business, acquiring new skills, or investing in different income streams, reinvesting ensures that your resources continue to work for you. It's about making your money grow rather than letting it stagnate or disappear.

Being wasteful is the quickest way to deplete your resources. Whether it's time, money, or energy, wastefulness can erode the foundation of your success. Keeping track of where your resources are going is essential. Monitor your expenses, evaluate your investments, and be mindful of how you spend your time. Every resource you have is valuable, and managing them wisely will set you apart.

As you manage your resources, remember that one of the strategies for growth is to let your money work for you. Money, when wisely invested, has the potential to generate more wealth. Instead of keeping your profits idle, put them to work through investments or expanding your business operations. This way, your money isn't just sitting there; it's actively contributing to your financial growth.

Delegating tasks is another crucial aspect of resource management. As your business grows, handling everything on your own becomes impossible. By trusting others to manage specific areas of your business, you free up your time to focus on strategic decisions that will drive your enterprise forward.

As you expand your business and manage your resources, it's crucial to remember the timeless principle of planting and harvesting. God provided manna to Israel during their journey to the Promised Land but allowed it to cease once they reached Canaan. The provision stopped so they wouldn't forget the necessity of planting and harvesting—a principle you must always keep in mind.

Jesus also demonstrated the importance of resource management when He gathered twelve baskets of leftovers after feeding the multitude. This act wasn't just about avoiding waste; it was a lesson in stewardship. Just as He ensured nothing was wasted, you must manage your resources carefully and diligently. Every profit, every opportunity, every resource you have should be treated with respect and used wisely.

As we draw this chapter and book to a close, I want to commend you for your dedication and commitment. You've taken a significant step by not just reading but by equipping yourself with the knowledge and tools needed to transform your life. However, knowledge alone is not enough—action is what brings results. Everything you've learned will remain dormant until you take that first step, and then the next, and so on. Remember, the oil in the widow's story didn't flow until she started pouring. Likewise, your transformation won't begin until you act.

I encourage you to apply the principles you've learned here. Don't let fear or doubt hold you back—your success is within reach if you're willing to pursue it with faith and determination. As you embark on this journey, know that I am here to celebrate your victories, no matter how small or big. Please reach out and share your success stories with me at toyin@pnuxelconsulting.com.

I look forward to hearing about your progress and celebrating your achievements.

I celebrate your courage and commitment and eagerly anticipate the great things you will accomplish. Cheers to your success!

Unlock Your Potential: Discover the Transformative Power of My Other Books

Are you ready to take control of your life and achieve your dreams? Look no further. In addition to **"FROM DEBT TO WEALTH: 12 Keys to Earn Money with What You Have,"** I have also written other books to help guide you on your journey to success.

"**FROM OVERWHELMED TO ORGANISED: A Time Management Blueprint for Busy Professionals**" reflects an insightful understanding of the challenges those leading demanding professional lives face. Drawing from personal experiences as a busy physician, author, coach, and digital solutions consultant, this book serves as a guide to take you from overwhelmed to organised.

"**LEVERAGING THE POWER OF SEASONS: Understanding and Taking Advantage of the Four Seasons of Life**" isn't just a book; it's a roadmap to unlocking the treasures and opportunities within the ever-changing seasons of life. This masterpiece will guide you to take advantage of these seasons to achieve great success.

"**FIND YOUR WORK: Unlocking Your Path to Impact, Fulfilment, and Worthy Compensation,**" is a guide to discovering the work you are wired to do, the kind that fills your soul with joy and fulfilment and impacts the world around you. It's about finding fulfilment and earning a worthy reward – not just financial rewards but also the intangible rewards money can't buy. So, if you're tired of feeling trapped in a job that drains you and craves a life of purpose and passion, then this book is for you. Pick up the book and let us find the work that brings joy and fulfilment because life is too short to spend doing anything less

In "**49 Words on Marble,**" I share wisdom and inspiration through powerful affirmations and motivational quotes for men and women, young and old. Positive mindset quotes to start your day and improve your life.

"**How to Live Above Circumstances**" teaches you how to be in control of your life and overcome any obstacle that may come your way. "**The Beatitudes**" explores the concept of living a life of happiness, prosperity, liberty, and blessedness.

In "**Write a Book Without Breaking a Sweat,**" I share the secrets to writing a book easily, making the process less daunting and more enjoyable. "**The Role of Graphic Design and Technology in Writing**" delves into the blogging world and how to develop a successful blog harnessing technology.

Each of these books offers unique insights and practical advice to help you navigate different aspects of your personal and professional life. Whether you're looking to cultivate a positive mindset, overcome challenges, manage your time effectively, or understand the different seasons of life, there's a book here to support you on your journey.

Take advantage of these transformative books. Check them out today by visiting my website [https://toyinobafemi.com.ng], Amazon store [https://www.amazon.com/Toyin-H.-Obafemi/e/B081TLJKH7], or search for them in your favourite bookstores.

The Author

Dr Toyin Obafemi is an author, coach, and medical doctor, currently serving as a Senior Registrar in Internal Medicine with an interest in Dermatology.

With a commitment to helping people live better lives, Dr Obafemi has authored more than ten impactful books published and distributed globally. One of his books, **"From Overwhelmed to Organized: A Time Management Blueprint for Busy Professionals,"** reflects an insightful understanding of the challenges those leading demanding professional lives face. Drawing from personal experiences as a busy physician, author, coach, and digital solutions consultant, this book has earned recognition as an Amazon best-seller.

Having once experienced what it meant to be on an unfulfilling job, Dr Toyin Obafemi understands that the human spirit yearns for something more — something that brings joy and fulfilment. That's why he has written his latest book, **"FIND YOUR WORK: Unlocking Your Path to Impact, Fulfilment, and Worthy Compensation,"** to help readers discover the work they are wired to do, the kind that fills their souls with joy and fulfilment. This book is about finding fulfilment and earning worthy rewards—not just financial rewards but also the intangible rewards money can't buy.

Beyond his professional pursuits, Dr Obafemi finds fulfilment in his role as a dedicated spouse to Temitope and a loving father to two children, Oreofe and Inioluwa. This holistic approach to life underscores his value on personal relationships and balance amidst his numerous commitments.

****

Thank you for reading this book. I will love to hear from you. Kindly send your feedback to toyin@toyinobafemi.com.ng or leave me a review at your favourite bookstore. Thanks

****

References

1. 2 Kings 4:1-7 One day the widow of a member of the group of prophets came to Elisha and cried out, "My husband who served you is dead, and you know how he feared the LORD. But now a creditor has come, threatening t | New Living Translation (NLT) | Download The Bible App Now [Internet]. [cited 2024 Sep 10]. Available from: https://www.bible.com/bible/116/2KI.4.1-7.NLT
2. Proverbs 13:22 NKJV - A good man leaves an inheritance to his - Bible Gateway [Internet]. [cited 2024 Sep 10]. Available from: https://www.biblegateway.com/passage/?search=Proverbs%2013%3A22&version=NKJV
3. 1 Peter 5:7 Give all your worries and cares to God, for he cares about you. | New Living Translation (NLT) | Download The Bible App Now [Internet]. [cited 2024 Sep 10]. Available from: https://www.bible.com/bible/116/1PE.5.7.NLT
4. Philippians 4 | NLT Bible | YouVersion [Internet]. [cited 2024 Sep 10]. Available from: https://www.bible.com/bible/116/PHP.4.NLT
5. Genesis 21 | NLT Bible | YouVersion [Internet]. [cited 2024 Sep 10]. Available from: https://www.bible.com/bible/116/GEN.21.NLT
6. Genesis 1:28 Then God blessed them, and God said to them, "Be fruitful and multiply; fill the earth and subdue it; have dominion over the fish of the sea, over the birds of the air, and over every living thing tha | New King James Version (NKJV) | Download The Bible App Now [Internet]. [cited 2024 Jun 15]. Available from: https://www.bible.com/bible/114/GEN.1.28.NKJV

7. Proverbs 4:23 Guard your heart above all else, for it determines the course of your life. | New Living Translation (NLT) | Download The Bible App Now [Internet]. [cited 2023 Nov 11]. Available from: https://www.bible.com/bible/116/PRO.4.23.NLT
8. Luke 19:13 So he called ten of his servants, delivered to them ten minas, and said to them, 'Do business till I come.' | New King James Version (NKJV) | Download The Bible App Now [Internet]. [cited 2024 Jun 15]. Available from: https://www.bible.com/bible/114/LUK.19.13.NKJV
9. Genesis 3:17 Then to Adam He said, "Because you have heeded the voice of your wife, and have eaten from the tree of which I commanded you, saying, 'You shall not eat of it': "Cursed is the ground for your sake; In | New King James Version (NKJV) | Download The Bible App Now [Internet]. [cited 2024 Jun 15]. Available from: https://www.bible.com/bible/114/GEN.3.17.NKJV
10. Genesis 1:5 God called the light Day, and the darkness He called Night. So the evening and the morning were the first day. | New King James Version (NKJV) | Download The Bible App Now [Internet]. [cited 2024 Jun 15]. Available from: https://www.bible.com/bible/114/GEN.1.5.NKJV
11. Genesis 1:31 Then God saw everything that He had made, and indeed it was very good. So the evening and the morning were the sixth day. | New King James Version (NKJV) | Download The Bible App Now [Internet]. [cited 2024 Jun 15]. Available from: https://www.bible.com/bible/114/GEN.1.31.NKJV
12. Genesis 2:5 before any plant of the field was in the earth and before any herb of the field had grown. For the LORD God had not caused it to rain on the earth, and

there was no man to till the ground | New King James Version (NKJV) | Download The Bible App Now [Internet]. [cited 2024 Jun 15]. Available from: https://www.bible.com/bible/114/GEN.2.5.NKJV

13. Genesis 1:26 Then God said, "Let Us make man in Our image, according to Our likeness; let them have dominion over the fish of the sea, over the birds of the air, and over the cattle, over all the earth and over ev | New King James Version (NKJV) | Download The Bible App Now [Internet]. [cited 2024 Jun 15]. Available from: https://www.bible.com/bible/114/gen.1.26

14. Ephesians 1:4 just as He chose us in Him before the foundation of the world, that we should be holy and without blame before Him in love | New King James Version (NKJV) | Download The Bible App Now [Internet]. [cited 2024 Jun 15]. Available from: https://www.bible.com/bible/114/eph.1.4

15. Daystar Christian Centre | Blossoming By The Help Of The Holy Spirit | 31st July, 2024 [Internet]. 2024 [cited 2024 Sep 10]. Available from: https://www.youtube.com/watch?v=HqAEdljcilo

www.ingramcontent.com/pod-product-compliance
Lightning Source LLC
Chambersburg PA
CBHW031619210526
45464CB00004B/1660